SPECTRUM®
Critical Thinking for Math
Grade 8

Published by Spectrum®
an imprint of Carson-Dellosa Publishing
Greensboro, NC

Spectrum®
An imprint of Carson-Dellosa Publishing LLC
PO Box 35665
Greensboro, NC 27425 USA

ISBN 978-1-4838-3556-3

03-223177784

Table of Contents Grade 8

Check What You Know

Integers and Exponents

Use the properties of exponents to fill in the blanks.

1. $(\underline{})^2 = \frac{25}{16}$

2. $5^{\underline{?}} = 1$

3. $8^3 \cdot \underline{} = 8^4$

4. $8^{\underline{?}} = \frac{1}{8}$

5. $(\underline{})^2 = 8^6$

6. $8^0 = \underline{}$

Solve the problems. Write each answer using scientific notation.

7. 3.4×10^4
   $+ 1.7 \times 10^3$

8. 3.4×10^4
   $- 1.7 \times 10^3$

9. 3.4×10^4
   $\times 1.7 \times 10^3$

10. 3.4×10^4
    1.7×10^3

11. The population of Sweden is about 9.4×10^6. The population of Switzerland is about 7.8×10^6. About how much larger is the population of Sweden? Write your answer in scientific notation.

Lesson 1.1 Proving Exponent Properties

Powers consist of a base number and an exponent.

$$\text{base}^{exponent} \qquad 2^4$$

The exponent tells how many times to multiply the base. This is called **expanded form**.

$$2^4 = 2 \cdot 2 \cdot 2 \cdot 2$$

When an expression contains multiple powers, there are certain properties that we need to know. The properties of exponents tell us how to operate with expressions that contain exponents.

Answer the questions to derive the **Product of Powers** property of exponents.

1. Write 3^2 in expanded form: _____

2. Write 3^4 in expanded form: _____

3. Write the product $3^2 \cdot 3^4$ in expanded form: _____

4. $3^2 \cdot 3^4 =$ _____

5. What is the relationship between the exponents of the factors and the exponent of the product?

6. Write a general rule for multiplying powers of the same base.

Lesson 1.1 Proving Exponent Properties

There are also properties for dividing powers and raising a power to a power. These properties can be used to evaluate expressions with exponents.

Answer the questions to derive the **Quotient of Powers** and **Power of Powers** properties.

1. Write the quotient $\frac{3^4}{3^2}$ in expanded form: _____

2. Use expanded form to divide $\frac{3^4}{3^2}$: _____

3. What is the relationship between the exponents of the dividend and divisor and the quotient?

4. Write the general rule for dividing powers of the same base.

5. Write $(3^4)^2$ as a product of 3^4: _____

6. Use the Product of Powers property to simplify your answer.

7. What is the relationship between the exponents in the original problem in #5 and the exponent in the final answer for #6?

8. Write a general rule for the power of a power.

Lesson 1.1   Proving Exponent Properties

Answer the questions to derive the **Power of a Product** and **Power of a Quotient** properties.

1. Write $(2 \cdot 3)^3$ in expanded form: _____

2. Write the answer using exponents: _____

3. What is the relationship between the exponent in #1 and the exponents in the answer for #2?

4. Write a general rule for the power of a product.

5. Write $\left(\frac{2}{3} \right)^3$ in expanded form: _____

6. Write the answer using exponents: _____

7. What is the relationship between the exponent in #5 and the ones in the answer for #6?

8. Write a general rule for the power of a quotient.

Lesson 1.2   Applying Exponent Properties

The properties of exponents explain how to operate with expressions that contain exponents.

Product of Powers
$$a^m \cdot a^n = a^{m+n}$$

Power of a Product
$$(a \cdot b)^m = a^m \cdot b^m$$

Power of a Power
$$(a^m)^n = a^{m \cdot n}$$

Zero Power
$$a^0 = 1$$

Quotient of Powers
$$\frac{a^m}{a^n} = a^{m-n}$$

Power of a Quotient
$$\left(\frac{a}{b}\right)^m = \frac{a^m}{b^m}$$

Negative Power
$$a^{-m} = \frac{1}{a^m}$$

Use the properties of exponents to complete the expressions. Name each property that you use.

$$4^3 \cdot 4^? = 4^5 \qquad\qquad (3 \cdot 4)^5 = 3^5 \cdot 4^? \qquad\qquad \frac{2^?}{2^2} = 2$$

$$\left(\frac{3}{7}\right)^3 = \frac{3^3}{7^?} \qquad\qquad 3^2 \cdot 3 = 3^? \qquad\qquad 15^? = \frac{1}{15}$$

$$(4 \cdot 2)^? = 1 \qquad\qquad \frac{1}{3^?} = 3^2 \qquad\qquad (12^?)^5 = 12^{-10}$$

Lesson 1.3 Scientific Notation in the Real World

Scientific notation is used to write very large or very small numbers. These numbers are written as an expression that shows a number between 1 and 10 multiplied by a power of 10.

$$34{,}000 = 3.4 \times 10^4 \qquad 0.00034 = 3.4 \times 10^{-4}$$

When adding or subtracting with scientific notation, the power of 10 must be the same. The decimal place can be moved to adjust the power of 10.

$$\begin{array}{r} 4.2 \times 10^7 \\ + \, 3.7 \times 10^5 \\ \hline \end{array} \qquad \begin{array}{r} 4.2 \times 10^7 \\ + \, 0.037 \times 10^7 \\ \hline 4.237 \times 10^7 \end{array}$$

When multiplying or dividing with scientific notation, add (after multiplying) or subtract (after dividing) the exponents of the 10s.

Answer the questions. Show your answers using scientific notation.

In 2010, the population in Brazil was 1.907×10^8 and the population in the Dominican Republic was 9.884×10^6. What is the total of the populations?

The population of a country is 1.79×10^8. A city in that country has a population of 1.25×10^6. How many times greater is the population of the country than the city?

Check What You Learned

Integers and Exponents

Use the properties of exponents to complete the following equations. Name each property that you used.

1. $\frac{5^?}{5^5} = 5^{-2}$

2. $(6^?)^4 = 6^{12}$

3. $\left(\frac{3}{8}\right)^? = \frac{3^2}{8^2}$

4. $\frac{6^5}{6^?} = 6^3$

5. $9^? \cdot 9 = 9^4$

6. $\frac{1}{10^?} = 10^2$

7. $(8^4 \cdot 8^6)^? = 1$

8. $8^? = 1$

Answer the questions. Show your answers using scientific notation.

9. The area of a state is 6.244×10^7 acres. A large ranch in the state covers 5.4×10^5 acres. What percentage of the state is covered by this ranch? Round your answer to the nearest thousandth.

10. A star has been receding at 4.2×10^{16} miles a year for 1.9×10^7 years. How far has it moved?

Check What You Know

Rational and Irrational Number Relationships

1. Classify each number as rational or irrational.

$\frac{1}{3}$ $0.\overline{3}$ 3π

3   −3 $\sqrt{3}$

2. Estimate the square root of each number.

$\sqrt{60} =$ $\sqrt{14} =$ $\sqrt{85} =$

3. Find the cube root of each number.

$\sqrt[3]{1} =$ $\sqrt[3]{125} =$ $\sqrt[3]{343} =$

4. Put the numbers in order from least to greatest on the number line.

$2\sqrt{5}$ $-\sqrt{8}$ $\frac{10}{6}$ -0.25

$2 + \sqrt{2}$ $\frac{\sqrt{60}}{2}$ $-1\frac{1}{3}$ $\frac{4}{5}$

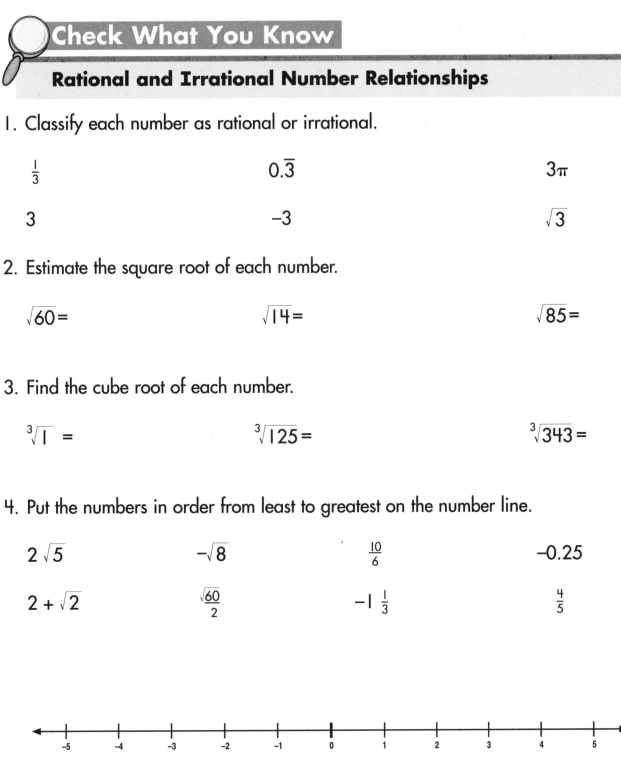

Lesson 2.1 Rational and Irrational Numbers

Note that the rational number classifications are nested. For example, a natural number is also a whole number, an integer, and a rational number.

Rational numbers can be expressed as ratios. This includes repeating and terminating decimals.

$$2, \frac{1}{2}, 0.\overline{2}, 0.5$$

Integers are all of the whole numbers and their opposites.

$$...-2, -1, 0, 1, 2...$$

Whole numbers are natural numbers and zero.

$$0, 1, 2, 3...$$

Natural numbers are also known as counting numbers.

$$1, 2, 3, 4...$$

Irrational numbers are decimals that never repeat or terminate.

$$0.1827658499.....$$

$$\pi, \frac{\pi}{2}, 2\pi$$

$$\sqrt{2}, \sqrt{8}$$

Name all of the classifications of the numbers.

44

$-\frac{10}{5}$

$\frac{1}{5}$

π

$\sqrt{5}$

0

Lesson 2.2 Square Roots

A perfect square is any number that shows the area of a square. The square root is the side length of that square.

$$\sqrt{9} = 3$$

You can estimate the square root of a number that is not a perfect square to estimate $\sqrt{42}$:

1. Find the nearest perfect squares to get a whole number estimate.
$$\sqrt{36} < \sqrt{42} < \sqrt{49} \; ; \; 6 < \sqrt{42} < 7$$

2. Find the differences between the lower perfect square and the number under the radical, as well as the difference between the two perfect squares.
$$42 - 36 = 6; \; 49 - 36 = 13$$

3. Find the ratio of the differences.
$$\frac{6}{13} = 0.462$$

4. Combine the square root of the lower perfect square and the decimal.
$$6 + 0.462 = 6.462$$

Estimate the square roots to the nearest thousandth.

$\sqrt{23}$

$\sqrt{210}$

Lesson 2.3 Cube Roots

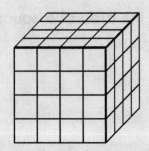 A perfect cube is any number that shows the volume of a cube. The cube root is the side length of that cube.

$$\sqrt[3]{64} = 4$$

You can estimate the cube root of a number that is not a perfect cube to estimate $\sqrt[3]{42}$:

1. Find the nearest perfect cubes to get a whole number estimate

$$\sqrt[3]{27} < \sqrt[3]{42} < \sqrt[3]{64} \; ; \; 3 < \sqrt[3]{42} < 4$$

2. Find the differences between the lower perfect cube and the number under the radical, as well as the difference between the lower and upper perfect cubes.

$$42 - 27 = 15; \; 64 - 27 = 37$$

3. Find the ratio of the differences.

$$\frac{15}{37} = 0.4$$

4. Combine the cube root of the lower perfect cube and the decimal.

$$3 + 0.4 = 3.4$$

Estimate the cube roots to the nearest tenth.

$\sqrt[3]{23}$ $\sqrt[3]{90}$

Lesson 2.4 Roots in the Real World

The play area in Rhonda's back yard is shaped like a square and has an area of 121 square feet. What is the length of the sides of the play area?

$$s^2 = 121; \sqrt{s^2} = \sqrt{121} ; s = 11$$

Each side is 11 feet long.

Solve the problems. Show your work.

The area of a square table top is 70 square inches. What are the dimensions of the table to the nearest hundredth?

Tasha is making a square mural. The area can be no more than 20 square feet. What is the longest length to the nearest tenth that each side can be?

Leah made some solid cube–shaped earrings. She used $\frac{27}{64}$ in.^{3} of wood for the earrings. How long was each side of each earring?

Lesson 2.5   Comparing and Ordering Numbers

Dexter's robot traveled $\sqrt{45}$ feet and Terri's robot traveled $5\sqrt{5}$ feet during a Robotics Club meeting. Dexter thinks that their robots traveled the same distance. Terri thinks that her robot traveled farther. Who is right? Justify your answer.

Dexter's Robot

$\sqrt{36} < \sqrt{45} < \sqrt{49}$

$6 < \sqrt{45} < 7$

$45 - 36 = 9$

$49 - 36 = 13$

$\frac{9}{13} = 0.69$

$6 + 0.69 = 6.69$ feet

Terri's Robot

$\sqrt{4} < \sqrt{5} < \sqrt{9}$

$2 < \sqrt{5} < 3$

$5 - 2 = 3$

$9 - 4 = 5$

$\frac{3}{5} = 0.6$

$2 + 0.6 = 2.6$

$5 \cdot 2.6 = 13$ feet

Terri is correct. Her robot traveled farther.

Students in Ms. Smalley's class recorded the number of minutes that they each spent on homework last night. Estimate each time to the nearest hundredth. Then, put the students in order from the one who spent the least amount of time on homework to the one who spent the most time on homework.

Jen: $24 + \sqrt{200}$

Adjoa: $11 \cdot \sqrt{75}$

Jorge: 12π

Abdul: $\pi \div \frac{1}{14}$

Order of students: _____

Check What You Learned

Rational and Irrational Number Relationships

1. List all of the classifications of the numbers.

   -3 $\qquad\qquad$ $0.\overline{6}$

   $\frac{1}{11}$ $\qquad\qquad$ 2π

   $\sqrt{13}$ $\qquad\qquad$ 47

2. Estimate each value to the nearest hundredth.

   $-2 \cdot \sqrt{54}$ $\qquad\qquad$ $12 + \sqrt[3]{12}$

3. Tommy wants to put a rug in a square room that has 775 square feet. He wants to leave a 3–foot border of bare floor on each side. What are the dimensions of the rug rounded to the nearest hundredth?

Check What You Learned

Rational and Irrational Number Relationships

4. The volume of a sphere is $V = \frac{4}{3}\pi r^3$. What is the radius of a sphere with a volume of 523.3 cubic meters? Use 3.14 for π.

5. The following times tell how many minutes each student ran either faster or slower than the average time. Put the students in order from fastest to slowest on the number line.

Shayla: $-\sqrt{3}$ Desean: $\frac{\sqrt{6}}{2}$ Tristan: $-\frac{7}{2}$ Valerie: $\frac{1}{3}\sqrt{12}$

Thomas: 3.5   Stacey: −0.25   Pam: $\frac{\sqrt{24}}{2}$ Jake: $\frac{\sqrt{36}}{4}$

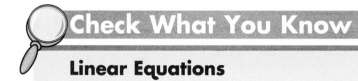

Check What You Know

Linear Equations

Solve the equations.

1. $3(2x - 1) + 4x = 25$

2. $5m - 3 = 2.5m - 21$

3. Liz and Zoe have the same number of baseball cards. Liz has 3 packs and 2 individual cards. Zoe has 2 packs and 10 individual cards. How many cards are in each pack?

4. What is the rate of change shown here?

x	3	5	8	10
y	4.5	7.5	12	15

5. What is the slope of the line?

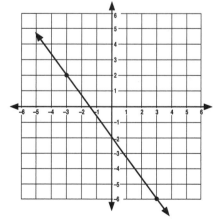

Check What You Know

Linear Equations

6. Graph the line: $y = -\frac{4}{3}x - 3$

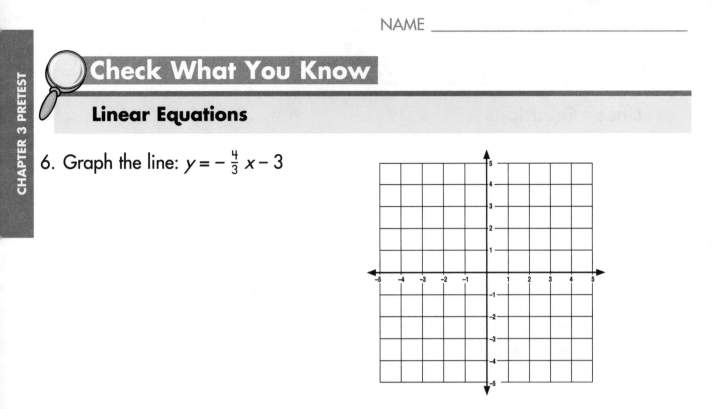

7. Graph the system of equations. Does it have one, no, or infinitely many solutions?

$y = \frac{3}{2}x - 2$

$y = -\frac{1}{2}x - 3$

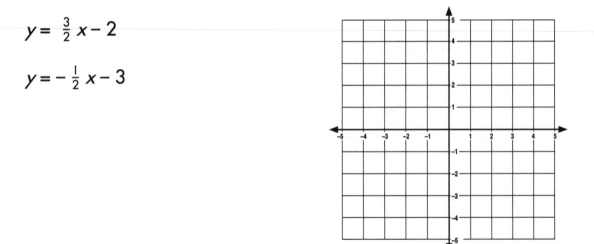

8. Solve by substitution:

$-2x + 2y = 2$

$y = 5x + 13$

Lesson 3.1 Equations with Variables on Both Sides

The iRead Book Club has a membership fee of $5 and charges $4 per book. The uRead Book Club has a membership fee of $4 and charges $5 per book. How many books would you need to buy for the total cost of both clubs to be the same?

Write an equation to represent each book club.
iRead: cost = $5 + 4b$ uRead: cost = $4 + 5b$, where b = number of books

Set the equations equal to each other and solve.

$5 + 4b = 4 + 5b$
$\underline{-5b -5b}$
$5 - b = 4$
$\underline{-5 -5}$
$-b = -1$

$\frac{-b}{-1} = \frac{-1}{-1}$
$b = 1$

The total costs would be the same if you buy 1 book from each club.

Solve the problems. Show your work.

A square and an equilateral triangle have the same perimeter. The length of the side of the square is $x + 10$. The length of the side of the triangle is $4x$. What is the length of the triangle side?

Abu is trying to decide which pet–sitting service he wants to use. Ur Pets charges a $15 fee, plus $1.75 per hour. Sit Pets charges an $11 fee, plus $2.25 per hour. At how many hours will both services charge the same?

Lesson 3.2 Analyzing Solutions of Equations

Some linear equations have multiple solutions or no solution.

One solution $x = a$	**Infinite solutions** $a = a$	**No solution** $a = b$
$4x + 8 = 4(2x + 1)$ $4x + 8 = 8x + 4$ $\underline{-8x \qquad -8x}$ $-4x + 8 = 4$ $\underline{-8 \quad -8}$ $-4x = -4$ $\dfrac{-4x}{-4} = \dfrac{-4}{-4}$ $x = 1$	$4x + 8 = 4(x + 2)$ $4x + 8 = 4x + 8$ $\underline{-4x \qquad -4x}$ $8 = 8$ True: any number will make the equation true.	$4x + 8 = 4(x + 1)$ $4x + 8 = 4x + 4$ $\underline{-4x \qquad -4x}$ $8 = 4$ False: no number can make the equation true.

Solve the equations. Show your work.

$-1.8 - 6x = 6(0.1 + 3x)$

$2.4m - 22 = -4(1 - 0.6m)$

$3(x - 1) - 1 = 3x + 2$

$-3(2x + 4) = \frac{1}{2}(4x + 8)$

Lesson 3.3 Representing Proportional Relationships

A proportional relationship is a constant ratio between quantities. This is called the constant of proportionality. It represents the rate of change, which is the ratio of the amount of change in the dependent variable (output) to the amount of change in the independent variable (input).

The table shows the relationship between time traveled and the distance traveled. Find the difference in values on each row of the table.

		+0.5	+1.25	+0.75
Time (hours)	1.5	2	3.25	4
Distance (miles)	93	124	201.5	248
		+31	+77.5	+46.5

$$\frac{\text{change in } y}{\text{change in } x} = \frac{31}{0.5} = \frac{77.5}{1.25} = \frac{46.5}{0.75} = \frac{62 \text{ miles}}{1 \text{ hour}}$$

The table shows a speed of 62 miles per hour.

Find the rate of change for the table.

Time (hours)	1.5	2	2.75	3.5
Distance from home (miles)	250	216	165	114

Lesson 3.3 Representing Proportional Relationships

You can use proportional relationships to find missing values in a table. Use the known rate of change to determine the missing values.

Time (hours)	1.5	2	?	4
Distance (miles)	108	?	234	288

Rate of change = $\dfrac{108}{1.5} = \dfrac{288}{4} = \dfrac{72 \text{ miles}}{1 \text{ hour}}$

$d = rt$
$d = 72(2)$

The distance is 144 miles in 2 hours.

$d = rt$
$234 = 72t$
$\dfrac{234}{72} = \dfrac{72t}{72}$
$3.25 = t$

The travel time is 3.25 hours for 234 miles.

Find the missing values.

Time worked (hours)	8	?	20.2	25
Pay earned (dollars)	$74	$111	?	$231.25

Lesson 3.4 Finding Slope Linear Relationships

Rate of change can also be found using a graph. The slope or rate of change is the ratio of change in the dependent variable and the change in the independent variable.

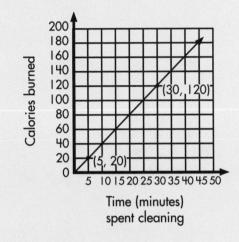

$$m = \frac{y_2 - y_1}{x_2 - x_1}$$

$(5, 20) \quad (30, 120)$

$$m = \frac{120 - 20}{30 - 5} = \frac{100}{25} = 4$$

4 calories are burned for each minute of cleaning.

Find the slope of each graph. What proportional relationship does the slope represent?

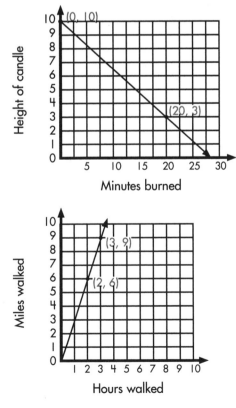

Lesson 3.4 Finding Slope Linear Relationships

Find the slope of each graph. What proportional relationship does the slope represent?

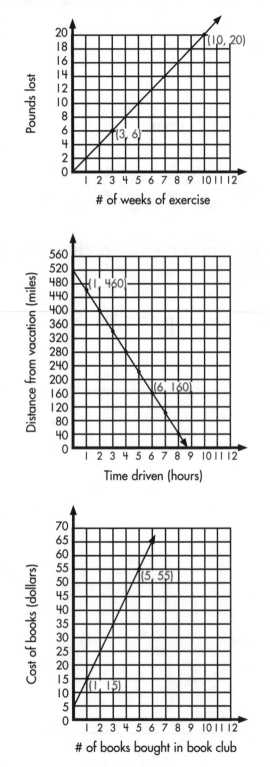

Lesson 3.5 Graphing a Line

The slope of a line represents the rate of change. The y-intercept is the point where the graph crosses the y-axis.

Graph and write the equation of the line that goes though the points $(-3, 2)$ and $(3, -6)$. Use the graph of the points to determine the slope. Use the line connecting the points to determine the y-intercept. What point with an x-coordinate of -9 would lie on the line?

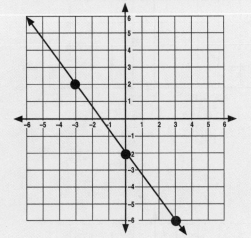

$$m = \frac{y_2 - y_1}{x_2 - x_1} = -\frac{8}{6} = -\frac{4}{3}$$

y-intercept = $b = -2$

slope intercept equation of a line:
$$y = mx + b; \ y = -\frac{4}{3}x - 2$$

when $x = -9$; $y = -\frac{4}{3}(-9) - 2$; $y = 12 - 2 = 10$
$(-9, 10)$

Graph the line and write the linear equation.

$(-1, 0)$ and $(1, 4)$

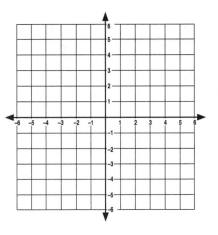

What point with an x-coordinate of -20 would lie on this line?

Lesson 3.5   Graphing a Line

Graph the lines and write the linear equation.

(−4, −3) and (0, 2)

What point with an *x*–coordinate of
14 would lie on this line?

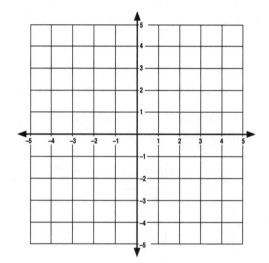

(3, −3) and (−4, 4)

What point with a *y*–coordinate of
−25 would lie on this line?

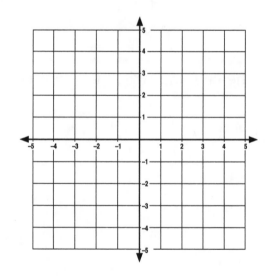

Lesson 3.6 Writing Linear Equations

Given 2 points, you can write a linear equation.
$$(-2, 0) \text{ and } (0, 1)$$

First, find the slope.
$$m = \frac{1 - 0}{0 - (-2)} = \frac{1}{2}$$

Choose 1 of the given points and the slope to find the y-intercept.
$$y = mx + b; \ 1 = (\tfrac{1}{2})(0) + b$$
$$1 = b$$

Write the equation.
$$y = \tfrac{1}{2}x + 1$$

Write the linear equation. What is the point on the line with a y-coordinate of 23?

$(-2, -1); (2, -5)$

Write the linear equation. What is the point on the line with an x-coordinate of 49?

$(2, -9); (-1, 3)$

Lesson 3.7 Linear Systems of Equations

A set of two or more equations that contain two or more of the same variables is a system of equations.

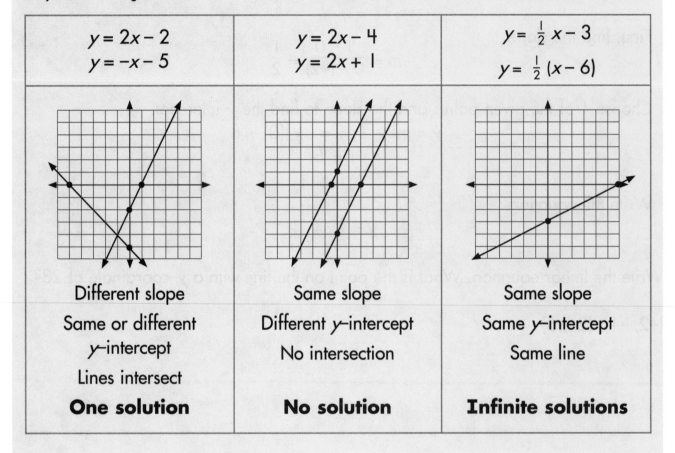

$y = 2x - 2$ $y = -x - 5$	$y = 2x - 4$ $y = 2x + 1$	$y = \frac{1}{2}x - 3$ $y = \frac{1}{2}(x - 6)$
Different slope Same or different y-intercept Lines intersect **One solution**	Same slope Different y-intercept No intersection **No solution**	Same slope Same y-intercept Same line **Infinite solutions**

State whether each system of equations will have one, no, or infinitely many solutions without graphing. Explain your thinking.

$y = -4x - 3$
$y = -2\left(2x + \frac{3}{2}\right)$

$y = -\frac{1}{4}x + 3$
$y = -\frac{1}{4}(x + 3)$

Lesson 3.7 Linear Systems of Equations

An ordered pair that satisfies both equations in a system of equations is considered a solution.

Does $(2,1)$ satisfy this system of equations? $\left\{ \begin{array}{l} y = 6x - 11 \\ -4x - 6y = -14 \end{array} \right\}$

Substitute the x and y into each equation to see if it is true:

$$1 = 6(2) - 11 \qquad\qquad -4(2) - 6(1) = -14$$
$$1 = 12 - 11 \qquad\qquad -8 - 6 = -14$$
$$1 = 1 \qquad\qquad\qquad -14 = -14$$
$$\textbf{True} \qquad\qquad\qquad \textbf{True}$$

The ordered pair satisfies **both** equations, so it is a solution.

Show whether each ordered pair is a solution to the system of equations.

$(0,-2)$

$-\frac{1}{2} x + 3y = -6$
$-5x + y = -2$

$(2, -3)$

$3x + 2y = 12$
$y = 5x - 7$

Lesson 3.8   Linear Systems in the Real World

Tracy has $20 in her bank account and saves $10 each week. Eric has $50 in his account and saves $5 each week. When will they have the same amount of money? How much money will they have then?

Tracy: $y = 20 + 10x$; Eric: $y = 50 + 5x$

Replace y in one equation with the value of y in the other equation.

$20 + 10x = 50 + 5x$
$\underline{\quad -5x \qquad -5x}$
$20 + 5x = 50$
$\underline{-20 \qquad\quad -20}$
$5x = 30$

$\dfrac{5x}{5} = \dfrac{30}{5}$
$x = 6$

They will have the same amount of money after 6 weeks.

$$y = 20 + 10(6) = 20 + 60 = 80$$

They will have $80 at 6 weeks.

Solve the problems. Show your work.

The length of a rectangle is 6 times the width. The perimeter is 84 meters. What is the length and the width? What is the area of the rectangle?

Tristan and Luke hiked a total of 18 miles in one weekend. Tristan hiked 6 miles more than Luke. How far did each person hike?

Lesson 3.8 Linear Systems in the Real World

Solve the problems. Show your work.

The sum of two numbers is 46. The second number is 4 less than the first. What are the two numbers?

Hamilton and Liam are saving money. Hamilton started with $10 and deposits $5 a week. Liam started with $5 and saves $5 a week. When will they have the same amount of money?

Valeria and Aiden are saving money. Valeria started with $10 and deposits $4 each week. Aiden started with $10 and makes two deposits of $2 each week. When will they have the same amount of money?

Check What You Learned

Linear Equations

1. Joey is training for a 5k race. She runs the same distance two days in a row. On the first day, she runs 5 laps around the track, and then runs an additional 1.5 miles. The next days she runs 3 laps, and an additional 4 miles. How long is each lap around the track?

2. Solve:

   $-4(3a + 3) + 14 = -12a - 9$

3. Solve:

   $3(6m - 4) + 8 = 2(9m - 2)$

4. Find the rate of change for the table. Explain what the rate of change represents.

Miles Driven	27	54	67.5	135
Gallons of Gas Remaining	14	13	12.5	10

Check What You Learned

Linear Equations

5. Find and interpret the slope:

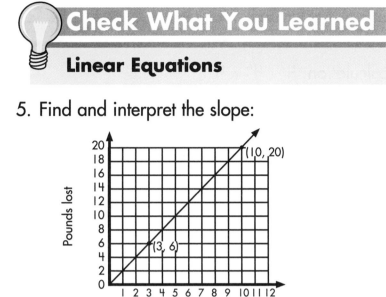

6. Does each system of equations have **one**, **zero**, or **infinite** solutions?

$$y = -\frac{4}{5}x + 3$$
$$y = -\frac{4}{5}x + 4$$

$$y = 2x + 1$$
$$y = \frac{1}{2}(4x + 2)$$

7. Is (0,–2) a solution for $\left\{ \begin{array}{l} -5x + y = -3 \\ 3x - 8y = 24 \end{array} \right\}$

Mid-Test Chapters 1–3

1. Find and explain the error in this calculation: $4^2 \cdot 4^6 = 4^{12}$

2. Find and explain the error in this calculation: $\dfrac{5^{45}}{5^{15}} = 5^3$

3. On average, there are 2.5×10^{13} red blood cells in the human body. There are 7×10^4 white blood cells. What is the ratio of red blood cells to white blood cells?

4. Human hair has an average diameter of 2.54×10^{-3} cm. If lighter hair has a diameter of 1.81×10^{-4} cm, what is the difference in diameter?

Mid-Test Chapters 1–3

5. Is $\sqrt{\frac{81}{16}}$ rational or irrational? Explain your reasoning.

6. Estimate the value of $\sqrt{175}$ to the nearest hundredth.

7. A cube has a volume of 220 cubic centimeters. What is the approximate length of each side?

8. Put the numbers in order from least to greatest.

$-\frac{1}{3}, -\sqrt{3}, 3.3, \sqrt{9}, \frac{\sqrt{30}}{10}$

NAME _____

9. Solve: $6(x + 3) - 10 = 2(3x + 4)$

10. Use the table to find the slope. What proportional relationship does the slope represent?

Number of Squats	5	10	15	20
Number of Bicep Curls	10	20	30	40

11. iOrange Music Service charges $4.95 for 5 songs and $19.80 for 20 songs. What is the cost per song? Is there a flat fee to subscribe to the service?

Mid-Test Chapters 1–3

12. There are 356 eighth–grade students at Euclid Middle School. 34 more than 4 times the number of girls is equal to half the number of boys. How many boys and girls are there at the school?

13. Solve by graphing.

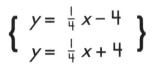

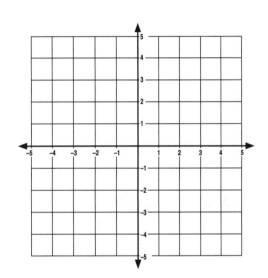

14. Is (−1, −4) the solution for $\left\{ \begin{array}{l} y = x - \frac{1}{2} \\ y = -\frac{1}{2}x - \frac{5}{2} \end{array} \right\}$?

NAME _____

Check What You Know

Functions

1. State whether the table shows a function.

x	y
1	−4
2	−5
3	−6
4	−7
2	4

2. What can be added or taken away from the table in problem #1 to make it a function?

Use the table to answer questions #3 – #6.

3. What is the rate of change in the table?

x	y
1	−4
2	−5
3	−6
4	−7

4. What is the initial value of this function?

5. Write a linear equation for this table.

Check What You Know

Functions

6. Make a graph of the function on page 40.

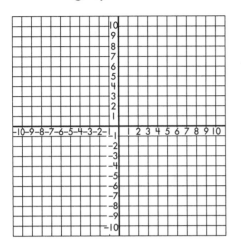

7. What might the function below be describing?

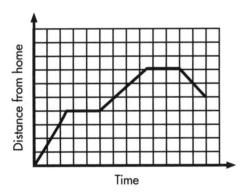

8. Classify the following function tables as linear or non-linear.

x	y
1	–4
2	–5
3	–6
4	–7

x	y
2	3
4	6
6	12
8	24

Lesson 4.1 Defining Functions

A function is a relationship where each input (independent variable) has exactly one output (dependent variable).

Is the relationship between a student's ID number and his or her name a function?

It is a function. Only one student is assigned to each ID number.

Is the relationship between the first and last names of students at a school a function?

It is not a function. Some students could have the same first name, but a different last name.

State whether each relationship is a function or not a function. Explain your answer.

The number of students and a teacher's 1st period class.

The number of charms on a bracelet and the cost of the bracelet if the empty bracelet costs $30 and each charm added to the bracelet costs $12.

A city and the state it is in.

The amount of time that you study and your test grade.

The length of the side of a square and the area of that square.

Lesson 4.2   Function Tables

You can create a table of values using a function.

Chanel earns $12 an hour at her job, plus a weekly laundry supplement of $15 to dry clean her uniform. Her weekly pay is represented by the function $y = 12x + 15$. She doesn't work the same number of hours each week. Create a table of values to represent her weekly pay for a variety of hours worked.

Hours Worked	$y = 12x + 15$	Weekly Pay
5	$y = 12(5) + 15 = 60 + 15$	$75
10	$y = 12(10) + 15 = 120 + 15$	$135
15	$y = 12(15) + 15 = 180 + 15$	$195
20	$y = 12(20) + 15 = 240 + 15$	$255

Create a table of values for each function.

The UText cell phone company charges a $40 access fee plus $10 per gigabyte of data used.

GB Used	$y = 10x + 40$	Total Bill
5		
10		
15		
20		

A plumber charges a $50 house call fee plus $35 an hour for plumbing repairs.

GB Used	$y = 35x + 50$	Total Bill
5		
10		
15		
20		

Lesson 4.2   Function Tables

You can also create a table of values using a graph of a function.

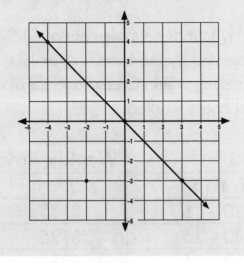

x	y
–4	4
–2	2
0	0
3	–3

The relationship between x and y: As x increases by 1 unit, y increases by 1 unit.

Create a table for each graph. Describe the relationship between x and y.

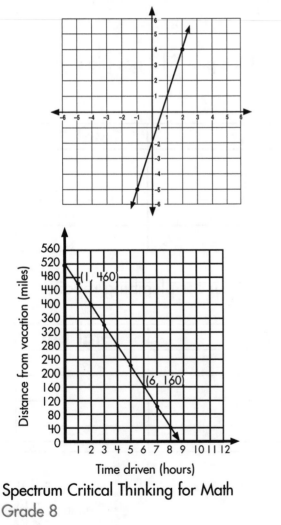

x	y

(1, 460)

(6, 160)

x	y

Lesson 4.3   Linear Functions

You can write a linear function using a table of values that have a linear relationship. Describe the graph of the function.

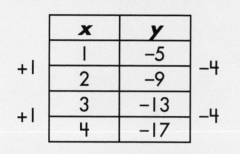

$m = \dfrac{\text{change in } y}{\text{change in } x} = \dfrac{-4}{+1} = -4$

Choose an ordered pair from the table: $(1, -5)$

Substitute into $y = mx + b$ to find b.

$-5 = (-4)(1) + b \qquad -5 = -4 + b$

$y = -4x - 1 \qquad\qquad \underline{+4 \quad +4}$

$\qquad\qquad\qquad\qquad\qquad -1 = b$

The graph of the function crosses the y-axis at -1. The y-values decrease by 4 as the x value increases by 1.

Write a linear function for the table. Describe the graph of the function.

x	y
-2	7
0	1
2	-5
4	-11

Lesson 4.3　Linear Functions

Write a linear function for each table. Describe the graph of the function.

x	y
2	-2
4	-4
6	-6
8	-8

x	y
-1	2
1	4
3	6
5	8

x	y
0	0
1	6.50
2	13
3	19.50

Lesson 4.4 Non-Linear Functions

A linear function has a constant rate of change. It will form a line when graphed. If the rate of change is not constant, then the function is non-linear. It will not form a line when graphed.

Determine if the following table is linear or non-linear

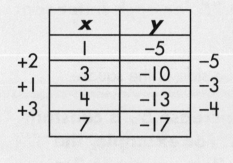

rate of change = $\dfrac{\text{change in } y}{\text{change in } x}$

$\dfrac{-5}{+2} = \dfrac{-4}{+3}$? $\dfrac{-5}{+2} \neq \dfrac{-4}{+3}$

The table is non-linear.

Determine if the functions are linear or non-linear.

x	y
−10	10
−5	4
0	2
5	0

x	y
1	0
3	−2
5	−4
9	−8

x	y
1	2
3	4
4	8
8	16

Lesson 4.4 Non-Linear Functions

If a description of a function indicates that the rate of change is constant, then it describes a linear function.

Hats R Us creates custom hats. It charges $7.50 for the hat and $0.75 for each letter that is stitched on the hat.

Linear. The cost of the hat increases by $0.75 for each letter that is stitched onto the hat.

The area of a square is the square of the length of one side of the square.

Non-linear. The area of a square doesn't increase by a constant amount as the length of the side increases. For example, the difference in area from a 1cm square to a 2cm square is $3cm^2$, but the difference from a 2cm square to a 3cm square is $5cm^2$.

Determine if each function is linear or non-linear.

The distance of the minute hand from the 12 on a clock as the minute hand moves around the clock.

The amount of protein in the can as Vince uses one scoop of protein power each day in his smoothie.

Parking fees if $2.00 is charged for the first hour, $1.00 is charged per hour for the 2nd through the 5th hour, and a flat fee of $5 is charged for more than 7 hours.

The number of bacteria being grown in a lab, if their number doubles every 2 hours.

Lesson 4.5 Rate of Change

Slope and rate of change are the same thing. Rate of change can be found using a table, graph, or equation. It can also be found using a written description.

Jessica has a t-shirt printing business. She charges a $30 design fee and $4 per t-shirt. What is the rate of change?

The cost increases by $4 for every t-shirt that is ordered.

Answer the questions.

After walking a mile, Vanessa starts jogging at a speed of 7 miles per hour. What is her rate of change each hour after she starts jogging?

Rebecca puts 10 gallons of gas in her car. She uses $1\frac{1}{4}$ gallons of gas for every 30 minutes that she drives. What is her rate of change for each hour?

At the basketball game, there are 50 students in the stands watching the game. 3 more students enter the stands every 2 minutes. What is the rate of change in the number of people entering the gym to watch the game?

Lesson 4.6 Initial Value

The y-intercept and initial value are the same thing. It can be calculated from a table, graph, or equation, or taken from a verbal description.

Jessica has a t-shirt printing business. She charges a $30 design fee and $4 per t-shirt. What is the initial value?

The initial cost of the t-shirts is $30 because Jessica will have to pay $30 no matter how many t-shirts she orders.

Find the initial value in each description.

Jennifer has 8 gallons of gas in her car. The amount of gas decreases by $1\frac{1}{3}$ gallons of gas for every 30 minutes that she drives.

Maria borrowed $75 from her father to buy concert tickets. She pays him back $20 every 2 weeks.

At the football game, 75 students are already in the stands watching the game, and 3 students enter the game every 2 minutes.

Dawn is driving home from her aunt's house, which is 45 miles away from her home. She is 10 miles closer to home for every 15 minutes that pass.

Lesson 4.7 Interpreting Functions

The meaning of a function can be interpreted by analyzing the rate of change and initial value of a function.

In the function $c = 25n + 20$, c is the cost of the cell phone bill, and n is the number of users on the phone plan. How much is charged for each user on the plan? What is the fee for having an account?

The cell phone bill is $25 per user on the plan, plus an account access fee of $20.

Answer the question about each function.

In the function $r = 2p + 50$, r is the number of rewards points at a video game store, and p is the amount of a store purchase. How many points does this customer already have?

Rewrite the equation for a customer who had 75 rewards points before he or she made the purchase.

In the function $s = 900 - 50w$, s is the amount in a savings account, and w is the number of weeks since school started. Jada worked all summer to save money that she could spend during the school year. How much does she spend each week?

How much did Jada save during the summer?

Lesson 4.7　Interpreting Functions

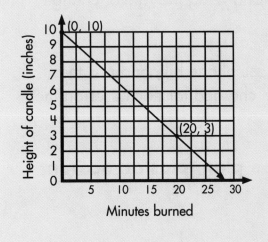

Use the graph to answer the questions.

What was the original height of the candle?
At 0 minutes, the height of the candle was 10 inches.

How fast is the candle burning?

$$\frac{3-10}{20-0} = \frac{-7}{20}$$

The height of the candle is decreasing by $\frac{7}{20}$ of an inch each minute.

Use the graphs to answer the questions.

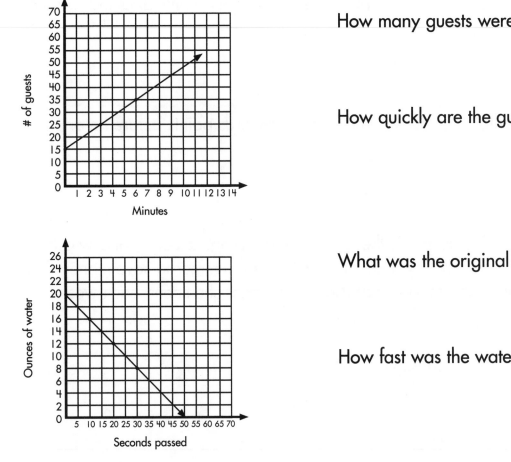

How many guests were already there?

How quickly are the guests arriving?

What was the original amount of water?

How fast was the water being consumed?

Lesson 4.8 Analyzing Functions

A graph can tell a story.

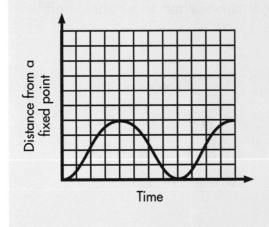

This graph shows the distance of an object from a fixed point. Describe the behavior of the graph.

The graph gets farther from the object, then gets closer, then gets farther again. The object seems to be moving in a circular motion near the fixed point.

Describe the behavior of each graph.

This graph shows the number of spectators at a basketball game over time.

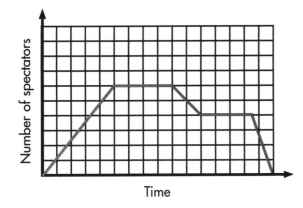

This graph shows the amount of money in a bank account over a period of weeks.

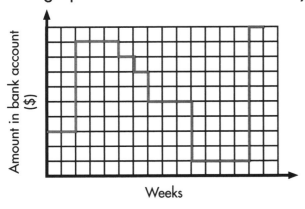

Lesson 4.9   Constructing Functions in the Real World

Write a linear equation to describe this relationship: $5°F = -15°C$ and $-40°F = -40°C$. Use it to find the Celsius temperature when the Fahrenheit temperature is $0°F$ and $60°F$.

$(5, -15)$ and $(-40, -40)$ are the ordered pairs. $\dfrac{-40 - (-15)}{-40 - 5} = \dfrac{-25}{-45} = \dfrac{5}{9}$

$$y = mx + b$$
$$-15 = \tfrac{5}{9}(5) + b$$
$$-15 = \tfrac{25}{9} + b$$
$$\dfrac{-\tfrac{25}{9} \quad -\tfrac{25}{9}}{}$$
$$b = -\tfrac{160}{9}$$
$$°C = \tfrac{5}{9}°F - \tfrac{160}{9}$$
$$°C = \tfrac{5}{9}(°F - 32)$$

$$0°F = ?°C$$
$$°C = \tfrac{5}{9}(0 - 32) = -17.78$$
$$0°F = -17.78°C$$

$$60°F = ?°C$$
$$°C = \tfrac{5}{9}(60 - 32) = 15.56$$
$$60°F = 15.56°C$$

Answer the question. Show your work.

Robert rents a van. He pays $105 when he drives 150 miles. Diane rents a van. She drives 100 miles and has to pay $80. Write an equation to represent the cost. What proportional relationship does the equation represent?

Lesson 4.9　Constructing Functions in the Real World

Answer the questions. Show your work.

DJ is training for a long-distance bike race. He starts recording his time and distance after he has already been riding for awhile. An hour later, he has traveled 24 miles and after 3 hours he has traveled 40 miles. Write an equation to describe the relationship.

What do the intercept and rate of change represent?

The boiling point of water is 213°F at 500 feet below sea level and 207.5°F at 2,500 feet above sea level. What is the boiling point at sea level?

Lesson 4.10 Comparing Functions

The table represents the balance on a loan that Jamie took out from her mother.

Time (weeks) since loan	Debt ($)
1	−80
3	−60
6	−30

Kenneth took a loan from his mother at the same time. The equation representing his debt is $y = 15x - 110$. Which person is paying their mother more money per week? Who took out the largest loan?

Jamie
$m = \frac{-60 - (-80)}{3 - 1} = \frac{20}{2} = \$10$

Jamie is paying $10 a week.

$y = mx + b$

$-30 = (10)(6) + b$

$-90 = b$

Jamie borrowed $90.

Kenneth
$m = 15$

Kenneth is paying $15 a week.

$b = -110$

Kenneth borrowed $110 from his mother.

Kenneth took out the largest loan and is paying back the most each week.

Tank A started with 9 feet of water and is being drained at 0.5 feet every 30 minutes. Tank B's drainage can be represented with the equation: $f = -0.75h + 10$, where f = feet of water and h = the number of hours that have passed. Which tank started with the most water? Which tank is draining faster?

Lesson 4.10 Comparing Functions

Answer the questions. Show your work.

Who needs the most Service Learning Hours: Tammy or Timmy? Who is volunteering the most hours each week?

Service learning hours Tammy needs:

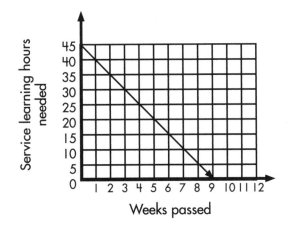

Service learning hours Timmy needs:

Weeks Passed	Service Learning Hours Needed
3	44
5	40
7	36
10	30

Check What You Learned

Functions

Use the table to answer the questions.

Wholesale Cost	Retail Cost
$9.50	$19.40
$12.50	$23.00
$14.00	$24.80
$20.00	$32.00

1. What is the rate of change shown in this table?

2. What is the initial value of this function?

3. Write a linear equation for the table.

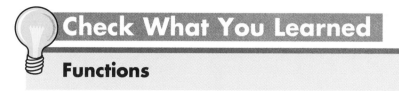

Check What You Learned

Functions

Use the table to answer questions 4 and 5.

4. What is the meaning of the rate of change and initial value for this table?

Wholesale Cost	Retail Cost
9.50	19.40
12.50	23.00
14.00	24.80
20.00	32.00

5. Make a graph of this function.

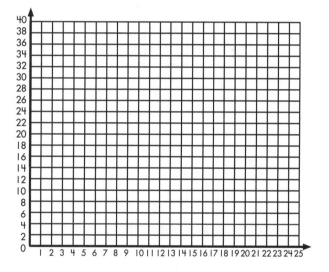

6. Zayn is filling a hole in the ground that is 30 inches deep. He is filling the hole at a rate of 3 inches in 15 minutes. The equation $h = -12x + 30$ represents the depth, h, of the hole after x hours. How long will it take for the hole to be half full?

Check What You Learned

Functions

7. This graph shows the speed of someone driving. What could be happening in the section of the graph where the speed is touching the *x*-axis?

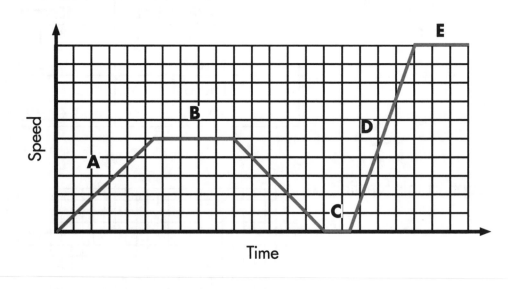

Identify the functions as linear or non-linear.

8. The radius and the volume of a sphere.

9. The number of hours worked and the amount earned.

10. The path of a basketball going into a basket.

NAME _____

Check What You Know

Geometry

1. Perform the following transformations on triangle ABC. Go back to the original △ABC before each transformation.

    a. Reflect over the *x*-axis

    b. Translate 4 units right and 3 units down.

    c. Rotate 180° about the origin.

    d. Dilate by a scale factor of 2 with the center of dilation at the origin.

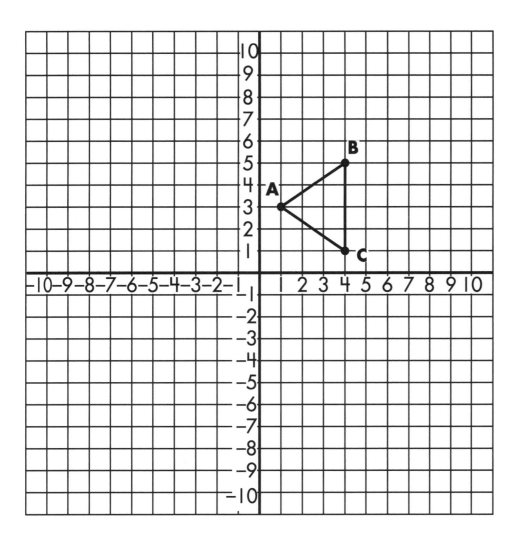

NAME _____

Check What You Know

Geometry

2. What angle(s) are congruent to ∠7?

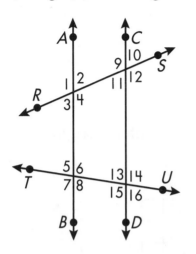

3. A right triangle has leg lengths of 6 cm and 8 cm. What is the length of the hypotenuse?

4. What is the volume of a cone with a radius of 3 cm and a height of 2 cm? Use 3.14 for π.

5. What is the volume of a sphere with a radius of 3 cm? Use 3.14 for π.

Lesson 5.1 Rigid Transformation

A translation is a transformation that slides a figure horizontally or vertically. It has the same size and shape as the image before the translations (pre-image).

Coordinates of pre–image:
$(x, y) \rightarrow (2, -1)$

Image after moving the pre-image left 3 units and up 2 units:
$(x', y') \rightarrow (x - 3, y + 2) \rightarrow$
$(2 - 3, -1 + 2) \rightarrow (-1, 1)$

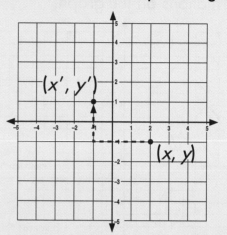

A reflection is a transformation that flips a figure across a line called the line of reflection. Each point reflected is the same distance from the line of reflection as the points of the pre-image. The image has the same size and shape of the image before the translations.

Coordinates of pre–image:
$(x, y) \rightarrow (2, -1)$

Image after being reflected over the x-axis:
$(x', y') \rightarrow (x, -y) \rightarrow (2, 1)$

Image after being reflected over the y-axis:
$(x', y') \rightarrow (-x, y) \rightarrow (-2, -1)$

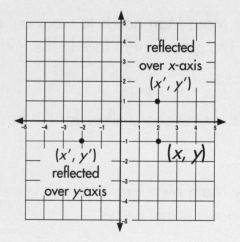

Lesson 5.1   Rigid Transformations

Video game designers use transformations to control the movement of game figures. Use the diagram of the game scene to answer the following questions. Show the transformations on the graph.

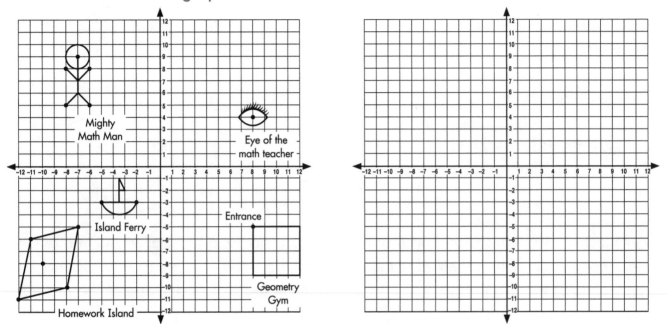

Mighty Math Man needs to work out at the Geometry Gym. What translation is needed to get his right foot to the entrance of the gym?

Write the new coordinates for the body if his right foot is at the entrance of the gym.

Mighty Math Man gets a power boost and reflects over the *x*-axis. What are the new coordinates of his body?

Mighty Math man goes back to his original location, then reflects (flips) over the *y*-axis. What are the new coordinates for his body?

Lesson 5.1 Rigid Transformations

A rotation is a transformation that turns a figure around a given point called the center of rotation. The image has the same size and shape of the image before the translations.

Coordinates of pre-image:
$(x, y) \rightarrow (2, -1)$

Image after being rotated 90° counterclockwise about the origin:
$(x', y') \rightarrow (-y, x) \rightarrow (1, 2)$

Image after being rotated 180° about the origin:
$(x', y') \rightarrow (-x, -y) \rightarrow (-2, 1)$

Image after being rotated 270° counterclockwise about the origin:
$(x', y') \rightarrow (y, -x) \rightarrow (-1, -2)$

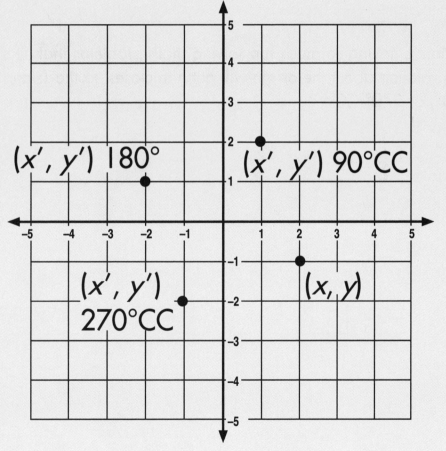

Lesson 5.1 Rigid Transformations

Use the game scene to answer the question. Show the transformations on the graph.

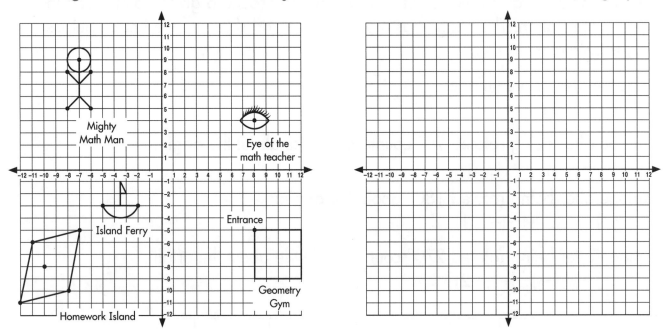

Mighty Math Man is having so much fun solving math problems that he spins around! Which rotation about the origin will get him closest to the Island Ferry: 90° CCW, 180°, or 270° CCW?

Lesson 5.2 Dilations

A dilation is a transformation that enlarges or shrinks a figure from a given point. It creates a similar figure. The image has the same shape as the image before the translations, but a different size.

Coordinates of pre-image:
$\triangle ABC$: A (2,−1), B (0,1), C (−1,−1)
Image after a dilation with the center of dilation at origin (where k is the scale factor):
$(kx, ky) \rightarrow (2x, 2y)$
$\triangle ABC$: A' (2 · 2, 2 · −1), B' (2 · 0, 2 · 1), C' (2 · −1, 2 · −1)
$\triangle ABC$: A' (4, −2), B' (0, 2), C' (−2, −2)

If $0 < k < 1$, image shrinks. If $k > 1$, image enlarges.

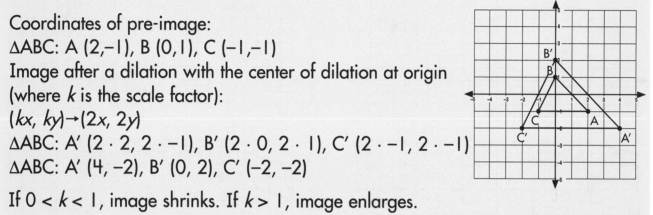

Use the game scene to answer the questions. Show your answer on the graph.

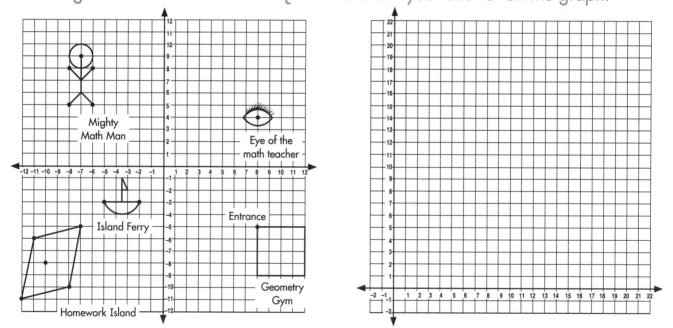

The Eye of the Math Teacher gets bigger when Mighty Math Man gets a problem right. The eye needs to grow by 2 because Mighty Math Man just got three problems right. What are the new coordinates of the center and each corner of the eye?

Lesson 5.2 Dilations

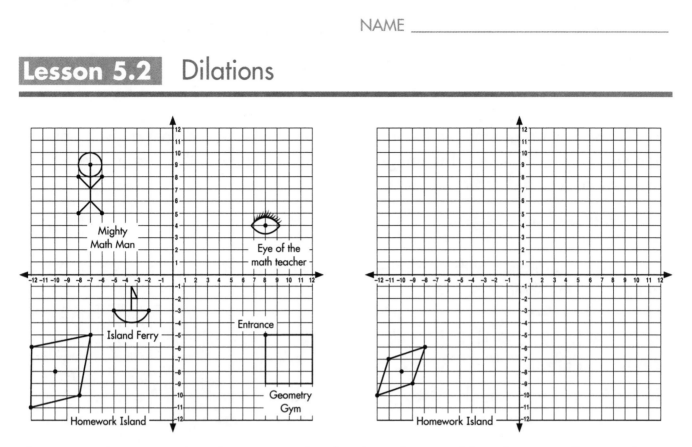

The game designers shrank Homework Island so they could make room for another feature. Did the game designers use a transformation to redraw the island, or did they just erase and redraw it?

The game designers want to make the Island Ferry smaller. What would be the new coordinates of the corners of the ferry if they reduced the size by 3?

Lesson 5.3   Sequence of Transformations

The game designer has decided to move the Geometry Gym and then make it larger.

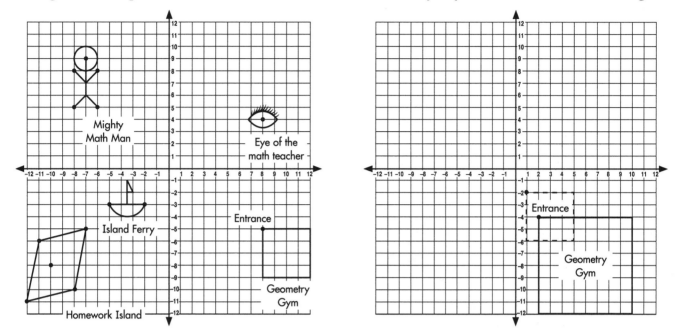

Describe the first transformation. Show what happened mathematically to the coordinates of the gym.

Describe the second transformation. Show what happened mathematically to the coordinates of the gym.

Lesson 5.3　Sequence of Transformations

The game designer wants to put Homework Island on the first quadrant.

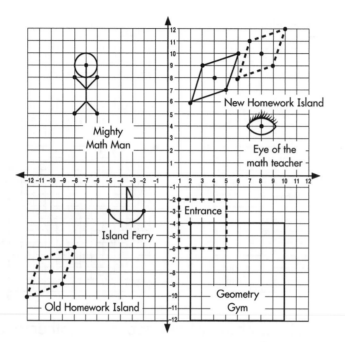

Describe the first transformation. Show what happened mathematically to the coordinates of the island.

Describe the second transformation. Show what happened mathematically to the coordinates of the island.

Lesson 5.4 Slope and Similar Triangles

You can use similar triangles to explain why the slope is the same between any two distinct points on a non-vertical line in the coordinate plane. Follow the directions below to prove that the slope is the same between any two distinct points on a line.

Draw a right triangle with the hypotenuse being the line segment between the points (−8,8) and (−6,6). What is the ratio of the length of the vertical leg to the length of the horizontal leg?

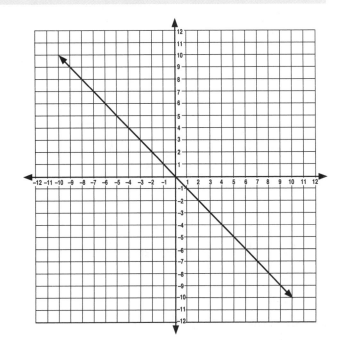

Draw a right triangle with the hypotenuse being the line segment between the points (−2,2) and (4,−4). What is the ratio of the length of the vertical leg to the length of the horizontal leg?

What is the relationship between the ratios of each of the triangles? Does this make the triangles similar or congruent?

Calculate the slope of the line. What is the relationship between the slope of the line and ratio of the lengths?

Lesson 5.5 Transversals and Calculating Angles

A transversal is a line that intersects two or more lines at different points. Angle pairs formed by the intersections are congruent. The angle pairs are:

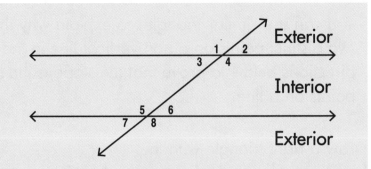

Angle Pairs	Examples
Alternate interior angles	∠4, ∠5; ∠3, ∠6
Alternate exterior angles	∠2, ∠7; ∠1, ∠8
Corresponding angles	∠1, ∠5; ∠3, ∠7; ∠2, ∠6; ∠4, ∠8

The relationships between parallel lines and their transversals can be used to justify the Triangle Sum Theorem. This theorem states that the sum of the angles of a triangle is 180°.

Extend the sides of the triangle to create transversals.

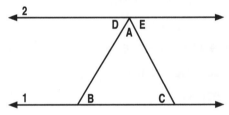

1. ∠D and what angle are alternate interior angles? _____

2. Since these two angles are alternate interior angles, they are _____

3. ∠E and what angle are alternate interior angles? _____

4. Since these two angles are alternate interior angles, they are _____.

5. ∠D, ∠A, and ∠E form a straight _____.

6. The angle measure of a straight line is _____°, therefore m∠D + m∠A + m∠E =

____

7. Using the relationships from #3 and #5, find the sum: m∠A + m∠B + m∠C=

____

8. The sum of the angle measures in a triangle is always _____

Lesson 5.5 Transversals and Calculating Angles

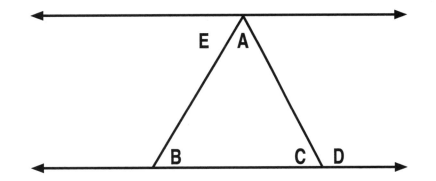

The relationships between parallel lines and their transversals can be used to justify the Exterior Angle Theorem. The Exterior Angle Theorem states that a measure of an exterior angle of a triangle is equal to the sum of the measures of the two non-adjacent interior angles.

Extend the sides of the triangle to create transversals.

What do $\angle$C and $\angle$D form? _____

What is the sum of the measures for $\angle$C and $\angle$D?

Set the sum of the interior angles equal to the sum of $\angle$C and $\angle$D since they both equal 180°. Simplify the equation.

Find the measure of each interior angle of the triangle, if $\angle$D = 105° and $\angle$E = 65°.

Lesson 5.6 Proving the Pythagorean Theorem

Use the image to answer the questions.

1. How are the squares related to the side of the triangle?

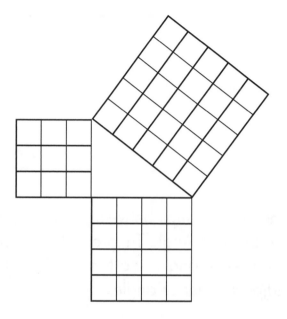

2. How are the areas of the squares related?

3. Write a general equation to represent the relationship that you described in #2.

4. If you used the same model for a triangle with legs of 9 units and 12 units, what would be the area of the third square?

Lesson 5.7 Triangles in the Real World

A painter is painting a tall wall. He has a 20-foot ladder that is 4 feet from the base of the wall. Is the ladder long enough for him to reach a spot that is 15 feet high on the wall?

The wall, ground, and ladder form a right triangle, so you can use the Pythagorean Theorem to find the length of the missing side. The Pythagorean Theorem states that $a^2 + b^2 = c^2$, where a and b are the lengths of the legs of a right triangle, and c is the length of the hypotenuse.

The hypotenuse is the side of the triangle that is opposite the right angle in the triangle.

$$a = 4 \text{ feet}; b = 15 \text{ feet}$$
$$4^2 + 15^2 = c^2; 16 + 225 = c^2$$
$$241 = c^2; \sqrt{241} = \sqrt{c^2}$$
$$15.5 = c$$

The ladder is long enough. It only needs to be 15.5 feet long.

Answer the questions. Show your work.

Phoebe cut across the soccer field to get to the parking lot, rather than walk along the perimeter of the field. If the field is 100 yards long and 50 yards wide, how much distance did she save by cutting across the field?

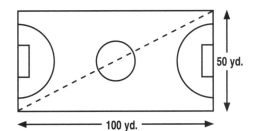

50 yd.

100 yd.

A pipe is being shipped in a long box that has a base of 2 ft. and a height of 8 ft. What is the longest length of pipe that can be shipped if it is put in the box diagonally?

Lesson 5.7 Triangles in the Real World

Answer the questions. Show your work.

Ronald and Donna both draw right triangles. The legs of Ronald's triangle are 4 cm and 5 cm. The legs of Donna's triangle are 3 cm and 6 cm. The sum of the legs of both their triangles is 9 centimeters, so they think that the hypotenuse of each of their triangles will be the same, too. Are they right?

Twins Rolanda and Yolanda are tired of sharing their bedroom. They want to split their 12 feet by 15 feet room diagonally with a curtain that is 18 feet long. Is the curtain long enough?

Lesson 5.8 Pythagorean Theorem and Distance

The Pythagorean Theorem can be used to find the distance between two points on a coordinate plane by using the horizontal and vertical distance between the points.

Find the distance between
the points (–2, 4) and (3, –4).
Horizontal distance: –2 – 3 = –5
Vertical distance: 4 – (–4) = 8

$(-5)^2 + 8^2 = c^2; 25 + 64 = c^2$
$89 = c^2; \sqrt{89} = \sqrt{c^2}$
$9.4 = c$

Use the map to answer the questions. A side of each square represents 2 yards.

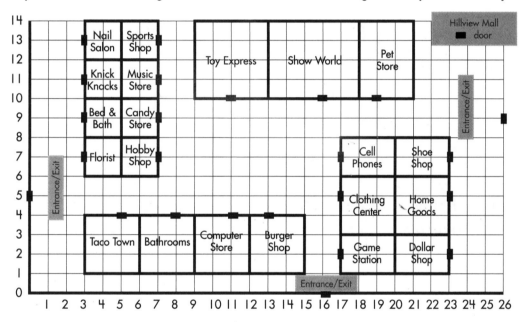

Travis walked diagonally from the cell phone store to the music store. How far did he walk? Round your answer to the nearest tenth of a yard.

After leaving the music store, Travis walks to the Computer Store. How far did he walk? Round your answer to the nearest tenth of a yard.

Lesson 5.9 Volume

Volume is the amount of space that a 3-D object can hold.

Figure	Volume Formula
Cylinder	$V = \pi r^2 h$
Cone	$V = \frac{1}{3} \pi r^2 h$
Sphere	$V = \frac{4}{3} \pi r^3$

Use the formulas to answer the questions. Use 3.14 for π.

Caleb has a cylinder that holds about 301 cm^3 of water. If the cylinder is 6 cm tall, what is the approximate radius?

John has a cone that has a radius of 4 inches. The cone can hold 105 in.^{3} of sand. What is the approximate height of the cone?

Jalisa is using water to fill a spherical balloon that has a radius of 9.4 cm. She has already used 1,000 cm^3 of water. Is the balloon more than half full?

Lesson 5.9 Volume

Use the formulas on page 78 to answer the questions. Use 3.14 for π.

A cylindrical tank with a radius of 4 feet and a height of 8 feet is being filled with a liquid. There is already 2 feet of the liquid in the tank. If more liquid is poured into the tank at a rate of 18 $\frac{ft.^3}{minute}$ for 15 minutes, approximately how high will the water be in the tank?

A cone shaped container is filled with sand. It has a radius of 4 inches and a height of 6 inches. The container has a small hole at the bottom and the sand is leaking out at a rate of 3.6 $\frac{in^3}{minute}$. After approximately how many minutes will the cone be empty?

A cylinder with a height of 12 cm and a diameter of 15 cm is being used to fill a 4874.85 cm^3 spherical tank with water. About how many times will the cylinder need to be filled in order to have enough water to fill the spherical tank?

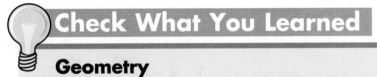

Check What You Learned

Geometry

1. Help the game designer change the game scene.
   a. Move the Super Plus down 4 and right 3.
   b. Reflect the gym over the y-axis.
   c. Reflect the Eye of the Math Teacher over the x-axis and dilate by a scale of $\frac{1}{2}$.

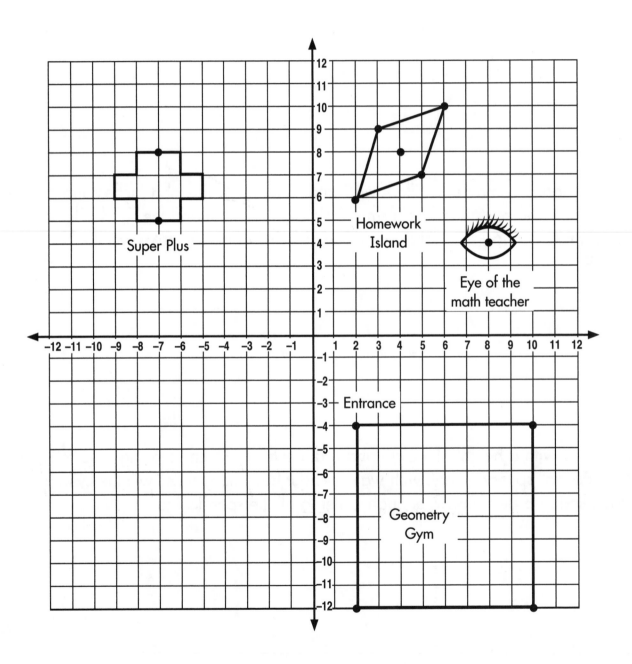

Check What You Learned

Geometry

2. What are the measures of ∠1, ∠2, and ∠3?

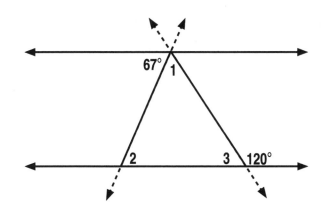

3. Television sizes are based on the length of the diagonal. If a 60-inch television has a width of 50 inches, what is the area of the television screen? Round your answer to the nearest tenth of a square inch.

4. A broom is leaning against the wall. It is 3.5 feet tall and its base is 6 inches from the base of the wall. How far up the wall is the top of the broom? Round your answer to the nearest tenth of a foot.

Check What You Learned

Geometry

5. Kobe wants to go to the gym with his friends. He started at Shaquille's house, then went to LeBron's house, and then went to the gym. If he traveled on a diagonal path, how far did he travel if each unit represents a city block? Round your answer to the nearest tenth.

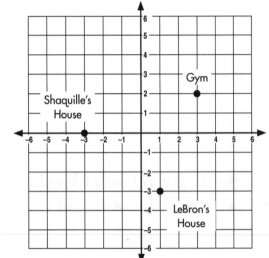

6. What is the total volume of the shape? Round your answer to the nearest hundredth. Use 3.14 for π.

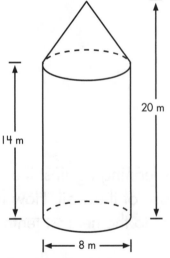

7. Linda is filling an ice bowl shaped like a hemisphere with a diameter of 10.4 inches. How much ice will fill the bowl? Round your answer to the nearest hundredth. Use 3.14 for π.

Check What You Know

Statistics and Probability

1. State whether the graphs show negative, positive, or no association.

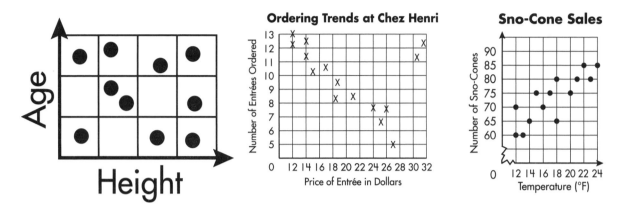

Ordering Trends at Chez Henri

Sno-Cone Sales

2. The table shows the relationship between the miles traveled for a trip and the cost of the trip. Create a scatter plot for the data.

Miles Traveled	Cost of Trip
450	460
120	290
250	330
310	410
60	240

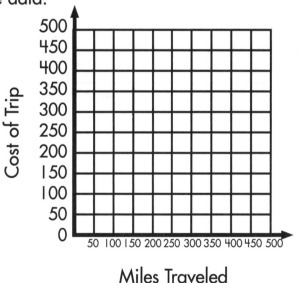

NAME _____

Check What You Know

Statistics and Probability

3. Draw a trend line.

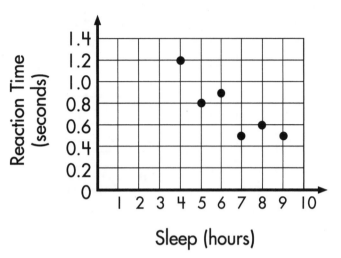

Sleep (hours)

4. What is the equation for the trend line?

5. Find the totals for the table.

	Favorite Color: Purple	**Favorite Color: Blue**	**Total**
Boys	25	60	
Girls	75	40	
Total			

Lesson 6.1 Interpreting Scatter Plots

A scatter plot is a graph with points plotted to show the relationship between two sets of data.

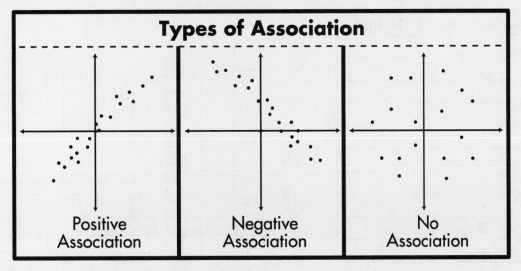

Answer the questions about the scatter plot.

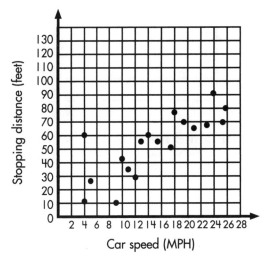

What is the type of association between car speed and stopping distance?

What is a possible explanation for this association?

Circle an outlier in this scatter plot, and explain what it might mean.

Lesson 6.2 Constructing a Scatter Plot

Use the table to create a scatter plot by graphing each ordered pair on the coordinate plane.

Reading Level	Height
1	45
2	50
3	45
3	51
4	55
4.5	65
5	60
6	64
6	70
6	90
6	71
8	76
9	72
10	85
11	100
12	95

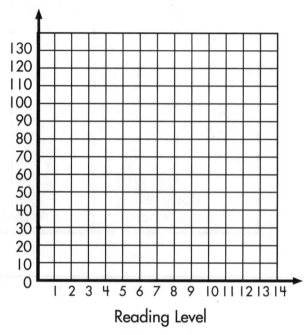

What is the relationship between a student's height and his or her reading level?

What is a reasonable explanation for why height would increase with an increase in reading level?

Lesson 6.3 Linear Models

A trend line shows the general direction that the points of a scatter plot seems to be going. The trend line of a scatter plot can be used to understand or make predictions about relationships between two variables.

Use the table to create a scatter plot by graphing each ordered pair on the coordinate plane. Draw a trend line through the data. Approximately half of the points should be above the line drawn, and the other half should be below it.

Age	Height
5	45
7	48
8	50
9	55
10	60
11	58
12	62
14	69
15	64

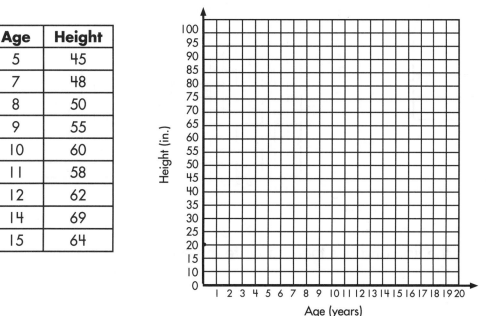

Pick two points on the line and use them to write the equation of the line.

What do the slope of the line and the y-intercept mean in the context of the problem?

Lesson 6.3 Linear Models

Use the table to create a scatter plot. Draw a trend line through the data. Approximately half of the points should be above the line drawn, and the other half should be below it.

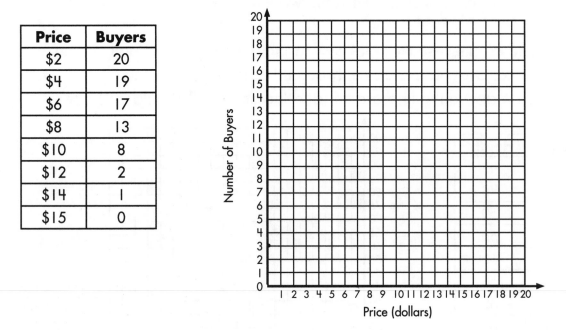

Price	Buyers
$2	20
$4	19
$6	17
$8	13
$10	8
$12	2
$14	1
$15	0

Pick two points on the line and use them to write the equation of the line.

What do the slope of the line and the *y*-intercept mean in the context of the problem?

Lesson 6.4   Scatter Plots in the Real World

The equation of a trend line can be used to make predictions.

The equation $y = 3x + 5$ is the trend line for a scatter plot of the number of questions on a test and the amount of time spent taking the test. Use the equation to predict how long it would take to take a test with 15 questions.

$$y = 3(15) + 5 = 45 + 5 = 50 \text{ minutes}$$

Students were asked how many hours they spent watching TV a week and what their math grade was. Their responses are shown on the scatter plot.

Pick two points on the trend line and use them to write the equation of the line.

Use the equation of the trend line to predict the expected grade of a student who watches 50 hours of TV a week. Round your answer to the nearest whole number.

Lesson 6.4 Scatter Plots in the Real World

The average speeds of cars during the Friday rush hour were recorded. Data collection started at 4:30 PM. Use the scatter plot to answer the questions.

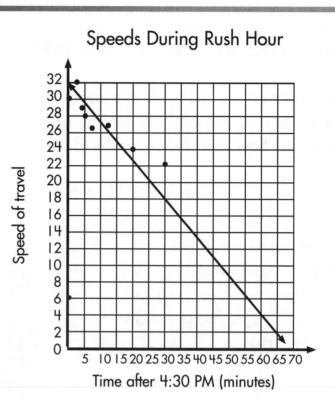

Speeds During Rush Hour

Pick two points on the trend line and use them to write the equation of the line.

Use the equation of the trend line to make predictions. Round your answer to the nearest mile.

a. How fast would a car be expected to travel at 4:45 PM?

b. How fast would a car be expected to travel at 5:30 PM?

Lesson 6.4   Scatter Plots in the Real World

Luis is training for a marathon. He records his mileage and time each day. Use the scatter plot to answer the questions.

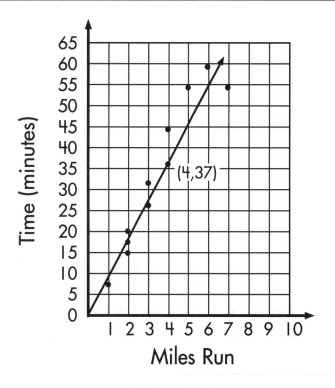

Pick two points on the trend line and use them to write the equation of the line.

What do the slope and *y*-intercept show?

Use the equation of the trend line to predict how far Luis could run in 25 minutes.

Lesson 6.5   Two-Way Tables

A two-way table shows data for two different categories. The table below shows the number of children who watch the TV shows "Dancing Stars" and "Zombie Nation."

	"Dancing Stars"	"Zombie Nation"	Total
Girls	30	10	
Boys	5	25	
Total			

How many students are represented?

30 + 10 = 40 girls and 5 + 25 = 30 boys: a total of 70 students. OR:

30 + 5 = 35 watch "Dancing Stars" and 10 + 25 = 35 watch "Zombie Nation": a total of 70 students.

What percentage of students are boys who watch "Zombie Nation"? $\frac{25}{70} = 35.7\%$

	Chores	No Chores	Total
Curfew	32	8	
No Curfew	2	8	
Total			

Use the two-way table to answer the questions.

Find the totals for the table.

What percentage of students have no chores and no curfew?

Lesson 6.5   Two-Way Tables

Use the two-way table to answer the questions.

	Football	Basketball	Total
Allergies	14	26	
No Allergies	31	9	
Total			

Find the totals for the table.

What percentage of students have allergies and like football?

Create a frequency table with the following information:

Mr. Neeley interviewed 100 eighth graders to see if they had 200 or more songs on their smartphones. He also noted if the student was a girl or a boy. Of the students, 20% had less than 200 songs, 40% were boys, and 50% of the boys had 200 or more songs.

	Less than 200 songs	200 or more songs	Total
Boys			
Girls			
Total			

Check What You Learned

Statistics and Probability

A class collected data to see if there was a relationship between shoe size and height.

Shoe Size	Height
5	55
6	62
12	72
10	71
8	69
11	70
7	64
11	72

1. Create a scatter plot with the data.

2. What is the equation of the trend line for this scatter plot?

3. What do the slope and *y*-intercept of the scatter plot represent?

Check What You Learned

Statistics and Probability

Use the equation for the trend line on page 94 to answer question 4.

4. Use the equation for the trend line to predict the expected height of a person who wears a size 9.

5. Create a frequency table with the following information:

Leonard interviewed 150 eighth graders to see if they would study for their math test. He also noted if the student had Ms. Brown or Mr. McCormick as a math teacher. Each teacher has the same number of students. Of the students, 50% said that they would study and 10% said they might study. 16% of Ms. Brown's students said they would not study, and none said they might study.

	Yes	No	Maybe	Total
Brown				
McCormick				
Total				

Check What You Learned

Statistics and Probability

	With Toppings	No Toppings	Total
Vanilla Ice Cream	9	8	
Chocolate Ice Cream	7	9	
Total			

Use the two-way table to answer the questions.

6. Find the totals for the table.

7. What percentage of students like vanilla with no toppings? Round your answer to the nearest percent.

8. Create a frequency table with the following information:

Mrs. Rakes interviewed 100 eighth graders to see if they preferred bowling or skating. She also noted if the student was a girl or a boy. Of the students, 42% like bowling, 48% were boys, and 25% of the boys preferred bowling.

	Skating	Bowling	Total
Boys			
Girls			
Total			

Final Test Chapters 1–6

Answer the questions. Show your work.

1. Shanise has 12 cubes that measure 12 units on each side. She says that the total volume of the cubes is 12×12^3. Juan disagrees and says that the total volume is 12^4. Who is correct?

2. The number of foreign travelers who visited New York City was 4.0×10^6 and the number that visited Boston was 7.2×10^5. How many times greater was the number of New York travelers than the number of Boston travelers? Round your answer to the nearest tenth.

3. Which is greater: $\sqrt{35}$ or $5\sqrt{7}$?

4. A square table cloth has an area of 1,600 square inches. It is placed on a table that has an area of 1,200 square inches. How much of the table cloth will hang over on each side? Round your answer to the nearest tenth of an inch.

Final Test Chapters 1-6

5. The iGo service charges a $10 fee to pick up a customer, and $0.10 per mile. uGo car service has no pickup fee, but charges $0.35 per mile. Find the number of miles for which the cost of both services is the same.

6. Harry is saving up for a game that costs $75. He has $28 in the bank. He saves $12 a week. The equation $s = 12w + 28$ represents how much he has saved after w weeks. How long will it take for him to earn enough for the game? Round your answer to the nearest week.

7. Does this equation have one solution, no solution, or infinitely many solutions?

$-3(x + 4) = -12 - 3x$

8. Does this equation have one solution, no solution, or infinitely many solutions?

$5(x - 2) + 3 = 5x - 9$

Final Test Chapters 1–6

9. The graph below represents the speed of a car over a given amount of time. Which section(s) of the graph represents a constant speed?

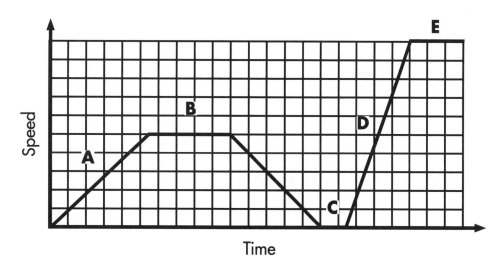

10. Compare the two functions:

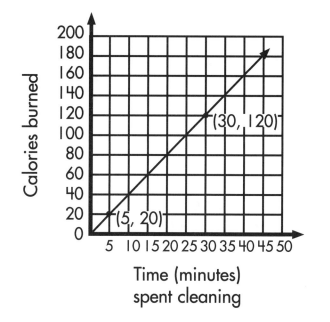

Time (minutes)
spent cleaning

$y = 7x$, where y is the number of calories burned when walking x number of minutes.

Final Test Chapters 1–6

11. What effect does a translation of $(x - 8, y + 10)$ have on the perimeter of a triangle?

12. What are the coordinates of a triangle with vertices A $(-1, 2)$; B $(8, -9)$; and C $(6, 1)$ after a rotation 90° clockwise about the origin?

13. Find the value of each angle of the triangle.

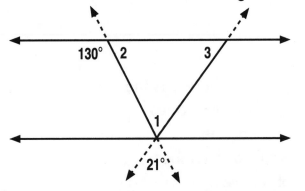

14. A boat's sail is shaped like a right triangle. If the leg of the sail is 12 feet and the hypotenuse is 20 feet, what is the length of the other leg?

CHAPTERS 1-6 FINAL TEST

Spectrum Critical Thinking for Math
Grade 8

100

Chapters 1–6
Final Test

Final Test Chapters 1–6

16. How much liquid can a sphere hold if it has a diameter of 12 centimeters? Round your answer to the nearest hundredth. Use 3.14 for π. Show your work.

17. Create a scatterplot for the data. Draw the trend line. What do the slope and *y*-intercept represent?

Hours Worked	Wages + Tips
2	16
3	21
4	22
2	10
5	30
3	19

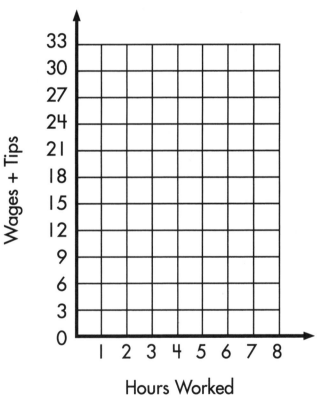

Answer Key

Page 4

Check What You Know

CHAPTER 1 PRETEST

Integers and Exponents

Use the properties of exponents to fill in the blanks.

1. $(\frac{5}{4})^2 = \frac{25}{16}$ 2. $5^? = 1$ $? = 0$

3. $8^3 \cdot 8^{\underline{8}} = 8^4$ 4. $8^? = \frac{1}{8}$ $? = -1$

5. $(8^{\underline{3}})^2 = 8^6$ 6. $8^0 = \underline{1}$

Solve the problems. Write each answer using scientific notation.

7. 3.4×10^4
$+ 1.7 \times 10^3$

3.4×10^4
$+ 0.17 \times 10^4$
$\overline{3.57 \times 10^4}$

8. 3.4×10^4
$- 1.7 \times 10^3$

3.4×10^4
$- 0.17 \times 10^4$
$\overline{3.23 \times 10^4}$

9. 3.4×10^4
$\times 1.7 \times 10^3$

$3.4 \times 1.7 = 5.78$
$10^4 \times 10^3 = 10^7$
5.78×10^7

10. 3.4×10^4
1.7×10^3

$3.4 \div 1.7 = 2$
$10^4 \div 10^3 = 10^1$
2×10^1

11. The population of Sweden is about 9.4×10^6. The population of Switzerland is about 7.8×10^6. About how much larger is the population of Sweden? Write your answer in scientific notation.

9.4×10^6
$- 7.8 \times 10^6$
$\overline{1.6 \times 10^6}$

Page 5

Lesson 1.1 Proving Exponent Properties

Powers consist of a base number and an exponent.

$$base^{exponent} \quad 2^4$$

The exponent tells how many times to multiply the base. This is called **expanded form**.

$$2^4 = 2 \cdot 2 \cdot 2 \cdot 2$$

When an expression contains multiple powers, there are certain properties that we need to know. The properties of exponents tell us how to operate with expressions that contain exponents.

Answer the questions to derive the **Product of Powers** property of exponents.

1. Write 3^2 in expanded form: $3 \cdot 3$

2. Write 3^4 in expanded form: $3 \cdot 3 \cdot 3 \cdot 3$

3. Write the product $3^2 \cdot 3^4$ in expanded form: $(3 \cdot 3) \cdot (3 \cdot 3 \cdot 3 \cdot 3)$

4. $3^2 \cdot 3^4 = 3^6$

5. What is the relationship between the exponents of the factors and the exponent of the product?
The exponent of the product is the sum of the exponent of the factors.

6. Write a general rule for multiplying powers of the same base.
$$a^m \cdot a^n = a^{m+n}$$
This is the Product of Powers property. Use it when multiplying powers of the same base.

Page 6

Lesson 1.1 Proving Exponent Properties

There are also properties for dividing powers and raising a power to a power. These properties can be used to evaluate expressions with exponents.

Answer the questions to derive the **Quotient of Powers** and **Power of Powers** properties.

1. Write the quotient $\frac{3^4}{3^2}$ in expanded form: $3 \cdot 3 \cdot 3 \cdot 3 \div 3 \cdot 3$

2. Use expanded form to divide $\frac{3^4}{3^2}$: $\frac{3 \cdot 3 \cdot 3 \cdot 3}{3 \cdot 3} = 3^2$

3. What is the relationship between the exponents of the dividend and divisor and the quotient?
The exponent of the quotient is the difference of the exponents of the dividend and the divisor.

4. Write the general rule for dividing powers of the same base.
$$\frac{a^m}{a^n} = a^{m-n}$$

5. Write $(3^4)^2$ as a product of 3^4: $3^4 \times 3^4$

6. Use the Product of Powers property to simplify your answer.
$$3^4 \times 3^4 = 3^{4+4} = 3^8$$

7. What is the relationship between the exponents in the original problem in #5 and the exponent in the final answer for #6?
The exponent of the answer is the product of the exponents in the original problem.

8. Write a general rule for the power of a power.
$$(a^m)^n = a^{m \cdot n}$$

Page 7

Lesson 1.1 Proving Exponent Properties

Answer the questions to derive the **Power of a Product** and **Power of a Quotient** properties.

1. Write $(2 \cdot 3)^3$ in expanded form: $(2 \cdot 3) \cdot (2 \cdot 3) \cdot (2 \cdot 3)$
$(2 \cdot 2 \cdot 2) \cdot (3 \cdot 3 \cdot 3)$

2. Write the answer using exponents: $2^3 \times 3^3$

3. What is the relationship between the exponent in #1 and the exponents in the answer for #2?
The exponent of the product is the same as the exponent of each of the factors.

4. Write a general rule for the power of a product.
$$(a \cdot b)^m = a^m \cdot b^m$$

5. Write $(\frac{2}{3})^3$ in expanded form: $\frac{2}{3} \cdot \frac{2}{3} \cdot \frac{2}{3}$

6. Write the answer using exponents: $\frac{2^3}{3^3}$

7. What is the relationship between the exponent in #5 and the ones in the answer for #6?
The exponent of the quotient is the same as the exponent of both the numerator and the denominator.

8. Write a general rule for the power of a quotient.
$$\left(\frac{a}{b}\right)^m = \frac{a^m}{b^m}$$

Answer Key

Page 8

NAME _____

Lesson 1.2 Applying Exponent Properties

The properties of exponents explain how to operate with expressions that contain exponents.

| **Product of Powers** | **Power of a Product** |
| $a^m \cdot a^n = a^{m+n}$ | $(a \cdot b)^m = a^m \cdot b^m$ |

| **Power of a Power** | **Zero Power** | **Quotient of Powers** |
| $(a^m)^n = a^{m \cdot n}$ | $a^0 = 1$ | $\frac{a^m}{a^n} = a^{m-n}$ |

| **Power of a Quotient** | **Negative Power** |
| $(\frac{a}{b})^m = \frac{a^m}{b^m}$ | $a^{-m} = \frac{1}{a^m}$ |

Use the properties of exponents to complete the expressions. Name each property that you use.

$4^3 \cdot 4^? = 4^5$
$? = 2$
Product of Powers

$(3 \cdot 4)^5 = 3^5 \cdot 4^?$
$? = 5$
Power of a Product

$\frac{2^?}{2^2} = 2$
$? = 3$
Quotient of Powers

$(\frac{3}{7})^3 = \frac{3^?}{7^?}$
$? = 3$
Power of a Quotient

$3^2 \cdot 3 = 3^?$
$? = 3$
Product of Powers

$15^? = \frac{1}{15}$
$? = -1$
Negative Power

$(4 \cdot 2)^? = 1$
$? = 0$
Zero Power

$\frac{1}{3^?} = 3^2$
$? = -2$
Negative Exponents

$(12^?)^5 = 12^{-10}$
$? = -2$
Negative Power

Page 9

NAME _____

Lesson 1.3 Scientific Notation in the Real World

Scientific notation is used to write very large or very small numbers. These numbers are written as an expression that shows a number between 1 and 10 multiplied by a power of 10.

$$34,000 = 3.4 \times 10^4 \qquad 0.00034 = 3.4 \times 10^{-4}$$

When adding or subtracting with scientific notation, the power of 10 must be the same. The decimal place can be moved to adjust the power of 10.

$$\begin{array}{r} 4.2 \times 10^7 \\ + 3.7 \times 10^5 \end{array} \qquad \begin{array}{r} 4.2 \times 10^7 \\ + 0.037 \times 10^7 \\ \hline 4.237 \times 10^7 \end{array}$$

When multiplying or dividing with scientific notation, add (after multiplying) or subtract (after dividing) the exponents of the 10s.

Answer the questions. Show your answers using scientific notation.

In 2010, the population in Brazil was 1.907×10^8 and the population in the Dominican Republic was 9.884×10^6. What is the total of the populations?

$$\begin{array}{r} 190.700 \times 10^6 \\ + 9.884 \times 10^6 \\ \hline 200.584 \times 10^6 \end{array}$$

$1.907 \times 10^8 \rightarrow 190.7 \times 10^6$

$200.584 \times 10^6 \rightarrow 2.00584 \times 10^8$

The population of a country is 1.79×10^8. A city in that country has a population of 1.25×10^6. How many times greater is the population of the country than the city?

$$\frac{1.79 \times 10^8}{1.25 \times 10^6} \qquad \frac{1.79}{1.25} = 1.432, \frac{10^8}{10^6} = 10^2$$

$$1.432 \times 10^2$$

Page 10

NAME _____

💡 **Check What You Learned**

Integers and Exponents

Use the properties of exponents to complete the following equations. Name each property that you used.

1. $\frac{5^?}{5^3} = 5^{-2}$
$? = 3$
Quotient of Powers

2. $(6^?)^4 = 6^{12}$
$? = 3$
Power of a Power

3. $(\frac{3}{8})^? = \frac{3^2}{8^2}$
$? = 2$
Power of a Quotient

4. $\frac{6^?}{6^1} = 6^3$
$? = 2$
Quotient of Powers

5. $5^? \cdot 9 = 9^4$
$? = 3$
Product of Powers

6. $\frac{1}{10^?} = 10^2$
$? = -2$
Negative Power

7. $(8^4 \cdot 8^6)^? = 1$
$? = 0$
Zero Power

8. $8^? = 1$
$? = 0$
Zero Power

Answer the questions. Show your answers using scientific notation.

9. The area of a state is 6.244×10^7 acres. A large ranch in the state covers 5.4×10^5 acres. What percentage of the state is covered by this ranch? Round your answer to the nearest thousandth.

$$\frac{5.4 \times 10^5}{6.244 \times 10^7} \qquad \frac{5.4}{6.244} = 0.865 \quad \frac{10^5}{10^7} = 10^{-2}$$

$$0.00865 \times 100 = 0.865\%$$

10. A star has been receding at 4.2×10^{16} miles a year for 1.9×10^7 years. How far has it moved?

$$(4.2 \times 10^{16})(1.9 \times 10^7)$$
$$4.2 \cdot 1.9 = 7.98$$
$$10^{16} \cdot 10^7 = 10^{23}$$
$$7.98 \times 10^{23} \text{ miles}$$

Page 11

NAME _____

🔍 **Check What You Know**

Rational and Irrational Number Relationships

1. Classify each number as rational or irrational.

$\frac{1}{3}$ $0.\overline{3}$ 3π
rational   rational   irrational

3 -3 $\sqrt{3}$
rational   rational   irrational

2. Estimate the square root of each number.

$\sqrt{60} =$ between 7 & 8 $\sqrt{14} =$ between 3 & 4 $\sqrt{85} =$ between 9 & 10

3. Find the cube root of each number.

$\sqrt[3]{1} = 1$ $\sqrt[3]{125} = 5$ $\sqrt[3]{343} = 7$

4. Put the numbers in order from least to greatest on the number line.

$2\sqrt{5}$ $-\sqrt{8}$ $\frac{10}{6}$ -0.25

$2 + \sqrt{2}$ $\frac{\sqrt{60}}{2}$ $-1\frac{1}{3}$ $\frac{4}{3}$

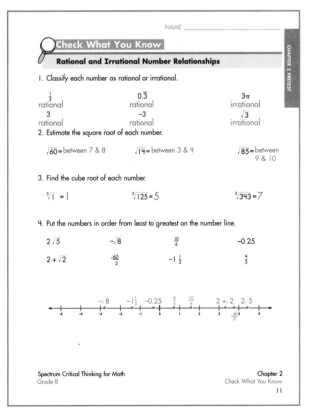

103

Page 12

NAME _____

Lesson 2.1 Rational and Irrational Numbers

Note that the rational number classifications are nested. For example, a natural number is also a whole number, an integer, and a rational number.

Rational numbers can be expressed as ratios. This includes repeating and terminating decimals.

$$2, \frac{1}{2}, 0.\overline{2}, 0.5$$

Integers are all of the whole numbers and their opposites.

...−2, −1, 0, 1, 2...

Whole numbers are natural numbers and zero.

0, 1, 2, 3...

Natural numbers are also known as counting numbers.

1, 2, 3, 4...

Irrational numbers are decimals that never repeat or terminate.

0.1827658499.....

$\pi, \frac{\pi}{2}, 2\pi$

$\sqrt{2}, \sqrt{8}$

Name all of the classifications of the numbers.

44	Natural, whole, integer, rational	π	Irrational
$-\frac{10}{5}$	Integer, rational	$\sqrt{5}$	Irrational
$\frac{1}{3}$	Rational	0	Whole, integer, rational

Spectrum Critical Thinking for Math
Grade 8
12

Lesson 2.1
Rational and Irrational Numbers

Page 13

NAME _____

Lesson 2.2 Square Roots

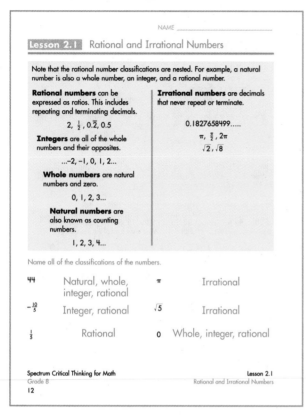

A perfect square is any number that shows the area of a square. The square root is the side length of that square.

$$\sqrt{9} = 3$$

You can estimate the square root of a number that is not a perfect square to estimate $\sqrt{42}$:

1. Find the nearest perfect squares to get a whole number estimate.

$$\sqrt{36} < \sqrt{42} < \sqrt{49} \; ; 6 < \sqrt{42} < 7$$

2. Find the differences between the lower perfect square and the number under the radical, as well as the difference between the two perfect squares.

$$42 − 36 = 6; 49 − 36 = 13$$

3. Find the ratio of the differences.

$$\frac{6}{13} = 0.462$$

4. Combine the square root of the lower perfect square and the decimal.

$$6 + 0.462 = 6.462$$

Estimate the square roots to the nearest thousandth.

$\sqrt{23}$

$$\sqrt{16} < \sqrt{23} < \sqrt{25}$$
$$4 < \sqrt{23} < 5$$
$$23 − 16 = 7$$
$$25 − 16 = 9$$
$$\frac{7}{9} = 0.778$$
$$4 + 0.778 = 4.778$$

$\sqrt{210}$

$$\sqrt{196} < \sqrt{210} < \sqrt{225}$$
$$14 < \sqrt{210} < 15$$
$$210 − 196 = 14$$
$$225 − 196 = 29$$
$$\frac{14}{29} = 0.483$$
$$14 + 0.483 = 14.483$$

Spectrum Critical Thinking for Math
Grade 8

Lesson 2.2
Square Roots
13

Page 14

NAME _____

Lesson 2.3 Cube Roots

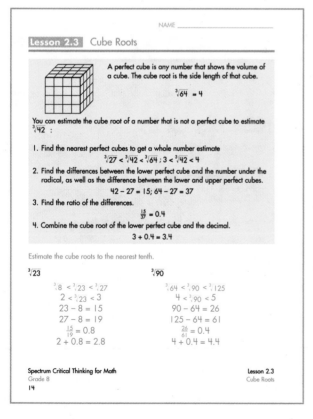

A perfect cube is any number that shows the volume of a cube. The cube root is the side length of that cube.

$$\sqrt[3]{64} = 4$$

You can estimate the cube root of a number that is not a perfect cube to estimate $\sqrt[3]{42}$:

1. Find the nearest perfect cubes to get a whole number estimate

$$\sqrt[3]{27} < \sqrt[3]{42} < \sqrt[3]{64} \; ; 3 < \sqrt[3]{42} < 4$$

2. Find the differences between the lower perfect cube and the number under the radical, as well as the difference between the lower and upper perfect cubes.

$$42 − 27 = 15; 64 − 27 = 37$$

3. Find the ratio of the differences.

$$\frac{15}{37} = 0.4$$

4. Combine the cube root of the lower perfect cube and the decimal.

$$3 + 0.4 = 3.4$$

Estimate the cube roots to the nearest tenth.

$\sqrt[3]{23}$

$$\sqrt[3]{8} < \sqrt[3]{23} < \sqrt[3]{27}$$
$$2 < \sqrt[3]{23} < 3$$
$$23 − 8 = 15$$
$$27 − 8 = 19$$
$$\frac{15}{19} = 0.8$$
$$2 + 0.8 = 2.8$$

$\sqrt[3]{90}$

$$\sqrt[3]{64} < \sqrt[3]{90} < \sqrt[3]{125}$$
$$4 < \sqrt[3]{90} < 5$$
$$90 − 64 = 26$$
$$125 − 64 = 61$$
$$\frac{26}{61} = 0.4$$
$$4 + 0.4 = 4.4$$

Spectrum Critical Thinking for Math
Grade 8
14

Lesson 2.3
Cube Roots

Page 15

NAME _____

Lesson 2.4 Roots in the Real World

The play area in Rhonda's back yard is shaped like a square and has an area of 121 square feet. What is the length of the sides of the play area?

$$s^2 = 121; \sqrt{s^2} = \sqrt{121} \; ; s = 11$$

Each side is 11 feet long.

Solve the problems. Show your work.

The area of a square table top is 70 square inches. What are the dimensions of the table to the nearest hundredth?

$$s^2 = 70 \qquad 70 − 64 = 6$$
$$\sqrt{s^2} = \sqrt{70} \qquad 81 − 64 = 17$$
$$s = \sqrt{70} \qquad \frac{6}{17} = 0.35$$
$$\sqrt{64} < \sqrt{70} < \sqrt{81} \qquad 8 + 0.35 = 8.35$$
$$8 < \sqrt{70} < 9 \qquad \text{Each side is 8.35 feet.}$$

Tasha is making a square mural. The area can be no more than 20 square feet. What is the longest length to the nearest tenth that each side can be?

$$s^2 = 20 \qquad 20 − 16 = 4$$
$$\sqrt{s^2} = \sqrt{20} \qquad 25 − 16 = 9$$
$$s = \sqrt{20} \qquad \frac{4}{9} = 0.4$$
$$\sqrt{16} < \sqrt{20} < \sqrt{25} \qquad 4 + 0.4 = 4.4 \text{ ft.}$$
$$4 < \sqrt{20} < 5$$

Leah made some solid cube-shaped earrings. She used $\frac{27}{64}$ in.³ of wood for the earrings. How long was each side of each earring?

Each side is $\frac{3}{4}$ inches.

$$s^3 = \frac{27}{64}$$
$$\sqrt[3]{s^3} = \sqrt[3]{\frac{27}{64}}$$
$$s = \frac{3}{4}$$

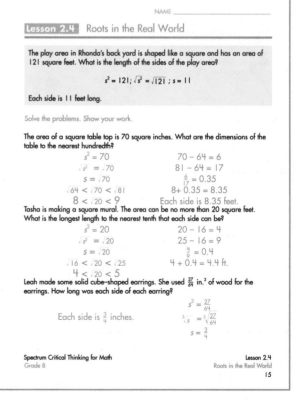

Spectrum Critical Thinking for Math
Grade 8

Lesson 2.4
Roots in the Real World
15

Page 16

NAME _____

Lesson 2.5 Comparing and Ordering Numbers

Dexter's robot traveled $\sqrt{45}$ feet and Terri's robot traveled $5\sqrt{5}$ feet during a Robotics Club meeting. Dexter thinks that their robots traveled the same distance. Terri thinks that her robot traveled farther. Who is right? Justify your answer.

Dexter's Robot
$\sqrt{36} < \sqrt{45} < \sqrt{49}$
$6 < \sqrt{45} < 7$
$45 - 36 = 9$
$49 - 36 = 13$
$\frac{9}{13} = 0.69$
$6 + 0.69 = 6.69$ feet

Terri's Robot
$\sqrt{4} < \sqrt{5} < \sqrt{9}$
$2 < \sqrt{5} < 3$
$5 - 2 = 3$
$9 - 4 = 5$
$\frac{3}{5} = 0.6$
$2 + 0.6 = 2.6$
$5 \cdot 2.6 = 13$ feet

Terri is correct. Her robot traveled farther.

Students in Ms. Smalley's class recorded the number of minutes that they each spent on homework last night. Estimate each time to the nearest hundredth. Then, put the students in order from the one who spent the least amount of time on homework to the one who spent the most time on homework.

Jen: $24 + \sqrt{200}$

$\sqrt{196} < \sqrt{200} < \sqrt{225}$
$14 < \sqrt{200} < 15$
$200 - 196 = 4$
$225 - 196 = 29$
$\frac{4}{29} = 0.14$
$14 + 0.14 = 14.14$
$24 + 14.14 =$
38.14 minutes

Adjoa: $11 \cdot \sqrt{75}$

$\sqrt{64} < \sqrt{75} < \sqrt{81}$
$8 < \sqrt{75} < 9$
$75 - 64 = 11$
$81 - 64 = 17$
$\frac{11}{17} = 0.65$
$8 + 0.65 = 8.65$
$11 \times 8.65 =$
95.15 minutes

Jorge: 12π
$12 \cdot 3.14$
37.68 minutes

Abdul: $\pi \div \frac{1}{14}$
$3.14 \cdot 14$
43.96 minutes

Order of students: Jorge, Jen, Abdul, Adjoa

Page 17

NAME _____

💡 **Check What You Learned**

Rational and Irrational Number Relationships

1. List all of the classifications of the numbers.

-3	Integers, rational	$0.\overline{6}$	Rational
$\frac{1}{11}$	Rational	2π	Irrational
$\sqrt{13}$	Irrational	47	Natural, whole, integers, rational

2. Estimate each value to the nearest hundredth.

$-2 \cdot \sqrt{54}$
$\sqrt{49} < \sqrt{54} < \sqrt{64}$
$7 < \sqrt{54} < 8$
$54 - 49 = 5$
$64 - 49 = 15$
$\frac{5}{15} = 0.33$
$7 + 0.33 = 7.33$
$-2 \cdot 7.33 = -14.66$

$12 + \sqrt[3]{12}$
$\sqrt[3]{8} < \sqrt[3]{12} < \sqrt[3]{27}$
$2 < \sqrt[3]{12} < 3$
$12 - 8 = 4$
$27 - 8 = 19$
$\frac{4}{19} = 0.21$
$2 + 0.21 = 2.21$
$12 + 2.21 = 14.21$

3. Tommy wants to put a rug in a square room that has 775 square feet. He wants to leave a 3–foot border of bare floor on each side. What are the dimensions of the rug rounded to the nearest hundredth?

$\sqrt{729} < \sqrt{775} < \sqrt{784}$
$27 < \sqrt{775} < 28$
$775 - 729 = 46$
$784 - 729 = 55$
$\frac{46}{55} = 0.84$
$27 + 0.84 = 27.84$
$27.84 - 3(2) = 21.84$
The rug is about 21.84 feet on each side.

Page 18

NAME _____

💡 **Check What You Learned**

Rational and Irrational Number Relationships

4. The volume of a sphere is $V = \frac{4}{3}\pi r^3$. What is the radius of a sphere with a volume of 523.3 cubic meters? Use 3.14 for π.

$523.3 = \frac{4}{3}\pi r^3$
$\frac{3}{4} \cdot 523.3 = \frac{3}{4} \cdot \frac{4}{3}\pi r^3$
$392.5 = \pi r^3$
$\frac{392.5}{\pi} = \frac{\pi r^3}{\pi}$

$125 = r^3$
$\sqrt[3]{125} = \sqrt[3]{r^3}$
$5 = r$
The sphere has a radius of 5 meters.

5. The following times tell how many minutes each student ran either faster or slower than the average time. Put the students in order from fastest to slowest on the number line.

Shayla: $-\sqrt{3}$ Desean: $\frac{6}{2}$ Tristan: $-\frac{7}{2}$ Valerie: $\frac{1}{3}\sqrt{12}$

Thomas: 3.5 Stacey: -0.25 Pam: $\frac{\sqrt{24}}{2}$ Jake: $\frac{\sqrt{36}}{4}$

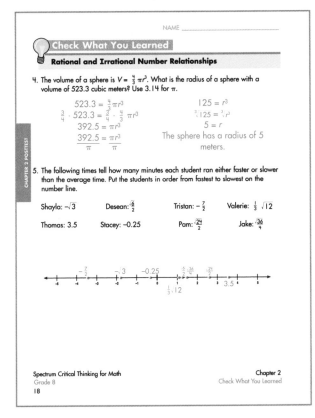

Page 19

NAME _____

🔍 **Check What You Know**

Linear Equations

Solve the equations.

1. $3(2x - 1) + 4x = 25$
$6x - 3 + 4x = 25$
$10x - 3 = 25$
$\underline{+3 \quad +3}$
$10x = 28$
$x = 2.8$

2. $5m - 3 = 2.5m - 21$
$\underline{-2.5m \quad -2.5m}$
$2.5m - 3 = -21$
$\underline{+3 \quad +3}$
$2.5m = -18$
$m = -7.2$

3. Liz and Zoe have the same number of baseball cards. Liz has 3 packs and 2 individual cards. Zoe has 2 packs and 10 individual cards. How many cards are in each pack?

$3p + 2 = 2p + 10$
$\underline{-2p \quad -2p}$
$p + 2 = 10$
$\underline{-2 \quad -2}$
$p = 8$

There are 8 cards in each pack.

4. What is the rate of change shown here?

x	3	5	8	10
y	4.5	7.5	12	15

$+2$ $+3$ $+2$ (top)
$+3$ $+4.5$ $+3$ (bottom)

$\frac{3}{2} = \frac{4.5}{3} = \frac{3}{2} \rightarrow$ The rate of change is $\frac{3}{2}$.

5. What is the slope of the line?

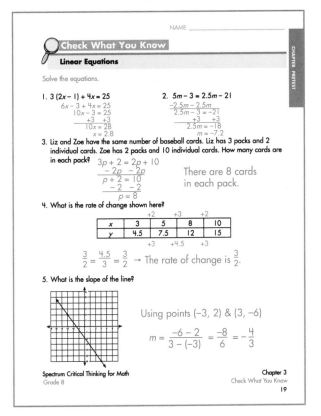

Using points $(-3, 2)$ & $(3, -6)$

$m = \frac{-6 - 2}{3 - (-3)} = \frac{-8}{6} = -\frac{4}{3}$

Page 20

Check What You Know

Linear Equations

6. Graph the line: $y = -\frac{4}{3}x - 3$

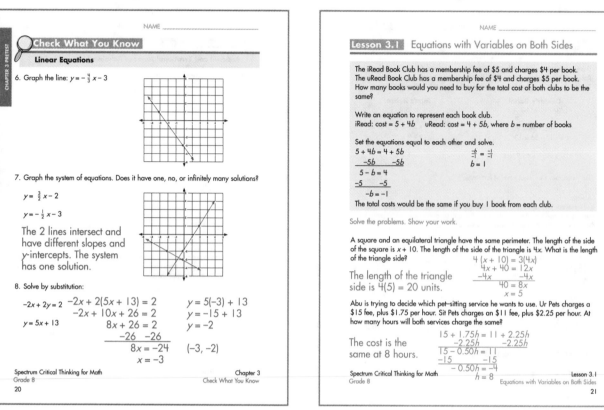

7. Graph the system of equations. Does it have one, no, or infinitely many solutions?

$y = \frac{3}{2}x - 2$

$y = -\frac{1}{2}x - 3$

The 2 lines intersect and have different slopes and y-intercepts. The system has one solution.

8. Solve by substitution:

$-2x + 2y = 2$

$y = 5x + 13$

$-2x + 2(5x + 13) = 2$
$-2x + 10x + 26 = 2$
$8x + 26 = 2$
$\underline{\quad -26 \quad -26}$
$8x = -24$
$x = -3$

$y = 5(-3) + 13$
$y = -15 + 13$
$y = -2$

$(-3, -2)$

Spectrum Critical Thinking for Math
Grade 8
20

Chapter 3
Check What You Know

Page 21

Lesson 3.1 Equations with Variables on Both Sides

The iRead Book Club has a membership fee of $5 and charges $4 per book. The uRead Book Club has a membership fee of $4 and charges $5 per book. How many books would you need to buy for the total cost of both clubs to be the same?

Write an equation to represent each book club.
iRead: cost = 5 + 4b   uRead: cost = 4 + 5b, where b = number of books

Set the equations equal to each other and solve.
$5 + 4b = 4 + 5b$
$\underline{\quad -5b \quad -5b}$
$5 - b = 4$
$\underline{-5 \quad -5}$
$-b = -1$

$\frac{-b}{-1} = \frac{-1}{-1}$
$b = 1$

The total costs would be the same if you buy 1 book from each club.

Solve the problems. Show your work.

A square and an equilateral triangle have the same perimeter. The length of the side of the square is $x + 10$. The length of the side of the triangle is $4x$. What is the length of the triangle side?

The length of the triangle side is $4(5) = 20$ units.

$4(x + 10) = 3(4x)$
$4x + 40 = 12x$
$\underline{-4x \quad\quad -4x}$
$40 = 8x$
$x = 5$

Abu is trying to decide which pet-sitting service he wants to use. Ur Pets charges a $15 fee, plus $1.75 per hour. Sit Pets charges an $11 fee, plus $2.25 per hour. At how many hours will both services charge the same?

The cost is the same at 8 hours.

$15 + 1.75h = 11 + 2.25h$
$\underline{\quad -2.25h \quad\quad -2.25h}$
$15 - 0.50h = 11$
$\underline{-15 \quad\quad -15}$
$-0.50h = -4$
$h = 8$

Spectrum Critical Thinking for Math
Grade 8

Lesson 3.1
Equations with Variables on Both Sides
21

Page 22

Lesson 3.2 Analyzing Solutions of Equations

Some linear equations have multiple solutions or no solution.

One solution $x = a$	Infinite solutions $a = a$	No solution $a = b$
$4x + 8 = 4(2x + 1)$ $4x + 8 = 8x + 4$ $\underline{-8x \quad -8x}$ $-4x + 8 = 4$ $\underline{\;-8 \quad -8}$ $-4x = -4$ $\frac{-4x}{-4} = \frac{-4}{-4}$ $x = 1$	$4x + 8 = 4(x + 2)$ $4x + 8 = 4x + 8$ $\underline{-4x \quad -4x}$ $8 = 8$ True: any number will make the equation true.	$4x + 8 = 4(x + 1)$ $4x + 8 = 4x + 4$ $\underline{-4x \quad -4x}$ $8 = 4$ False: no number can make the equation true.

Solve the equations. Show your work.

$-1.8 - 6x = 6(0.1 + 3x)$
$-1.8 - 6x = 0.6 + 18x$
$\underline{\quad -18x \quad -18x}$
$-1.8 - 24x = 0.6$
$\underline{+1.8 \quad\quad +1.8}$
$-24x = 2.4$
$x = -0.1$

$2.4m - 22 = -4(1 - 0.6m)$
$2.4m - 22 = -4 + 2.4m$
$\underline{-2.4m \quad\quad -2.4m}$
$-22 = -4$
No solution

$3(x - 1) - 1 = 3x + 2$
$3x - 3 - 1 = 3x + 2$
$3x - 4 = 3x + 2$
$\underline{-3x \quad\quad -3x}$
$-4 = 2$
No solution

$-3(2x + 4) = \frac{1}{2}(4x + 8)$
$-6x - 12 = 2x + 4$
$\underline{-2x \quad\quad -2x}$
$-8x - 12 = 4$
$\underline{\quad +12 \quad +12}$
$-8x = 16$
$x = -2$

Spectrum Critical Thinking for Math
Grade 8
22

Lesson 3.2
Analyzing Solutions of Equations

Page 23

Lesson 3.3 Representing Proportional Relationships

A proportional relationship is a constant ratio between quantities. This is called the constant of proportionality. It represents the rate of change, which is the ratio of the amount of change in the dependent variable (output) to the amount of change in the independent variable (input).

The table shows the relationship between time traveled and the distance traveled. Find the difference in values on each row of the table.

	+0.5	+1.25	+0.75
Time (hours)	1.5	2	3.25	4
Distance (miles)	93	124	201.5	248
	+31	+77.5	+46.5

$\frac{\text{change in } y}{\text{change in } x} = \frac{31}{0.5} = \frac{77.5}{1.25} = \frac{46.5}{0.75} = \frac{62 \text{ miles}}{1 \text{ hour}}$

The table shows a speed of 62 miles per hour.

Find the rate of change for the table.

	+0.5	+0.75	+0.75
Time (hours)	1.5	2	2.75	3.5
Distance from home (miles)	250	216	165	114
	-34	-51	-51

$-\frac{34}{0.5} = -\frac{51}{0.75} = -\frac{51}{0.75} = -\frac{68 \text{ miles}}{1 \text{ hour}}$

The person is getting 68 miles closer to home per hour.

Spectrum Critical Thinking for Math
Grade 8

Lesson 3.3
Representing Proportional Relationships
23

Page 24

NAME _____

Lesson 3.3 Representing Proportional Relationships

You can use proportional relationships to find missing values in a table. Use the known rate of change to determine the missing values.

Time (hours)	1.5	2	?	4
Distance (miles)	108	?	234	288

Rate of change = $\frac{108}{1.5} = \frac{288}{4} = \frac{72 \text{ miles}}{1 \text{ hour}}$

$d = rt$
$d = 72(2)$

The distance is 144 miles in 2 hours.

$d = rt$
$234 = 72t$
$\frac{234}{72} = \frac{72t}{72}$
$3.25 = t$

The travel time is 3.25 hours for 234 miles.

Find the missing values.

Time worked (hours)	8	?	20.2	25
Pay earned (dollars)	$74	$111	?	$231.25

rate of change = $\frac{74}{8} = \frac{231.25}{25} = \frac{\$9.25}{\text{hours worked}}$

pay = hourly rate · hours worked
$111 = 9.25 \cdot h$
$\frac{111}{9.25} = \frac{9.25h}{9.25}$
$12 = h$
If the pay is $111, 12 hours were worked.

pay = hourly rate · hours worked
pay = 9.25 · 20.2
pay = 186.85
The pay is $186.85 for 20.2 hours worked.

Spectrum Critical Thinking for Math
Grade 8
24

Lesson 3.3
Representing Proportional Relationships

Page 25

NAME _____

Lesson 3.4 Finding Slope Linear Relationships

Rate of change can also be found using a graph. The slope or rate of change is the ratio of change in the dependent variable and the change in the independent variable.

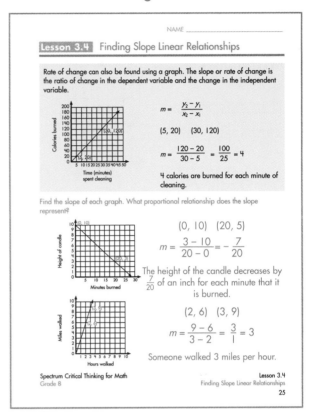

$m = \frac{y_2 - y_1}{x_2 - x_1}$

$(5, 20) \quad (30, 120)$

$m = \frac{120 - 20}{30 - 5} = \frac{100}{25} = 4$

4 calories are burned for each minute of cleaning.

Find the slope of each graph. What proportional relationship does the slope represent?

$(0, 10) \quad (20, 5)$

$m = \frac{3 - 10}{20 - 0} = -\frac{7}{20}$

The height of the candle decreases by $\frac{7}{20}$ of an inch for each minute that it is burned.

$(2, 6) \quad (3, 9)$

$m = \frac{9 - 6}{3 - 2} = \frac{3}{1} = 3$

Someone walked 3 miles per hour.

Spectrum Critical Thinking for Math
Grade 8

Lesson 3.4
Finding Slope Linear Relationships
25

Page 26

NAME _____

Lesson 3.4 Finding Slope Linear Relationships

Find the slope of each graph. What proportional relationship does the slope represent?

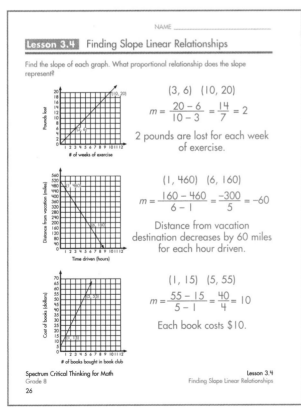

$(3, 6) \quad (10, 20)$

$m = \frac{20 - 6}{10 - 3} = \frac{14}{7} = 2$

2 pounds are lost for each week of exercise.

$(1, 460) \quad (6, 160)$

$m = \frac{160 - 460}{6 - 1} = \frac{-300}{5} = -60$

Distance from vacation destination decreases by 60 miles for each hour driven.

$(1, 15) \quad (5, 55)$

$m = \frac{55 - 15}{5 - 1} = \frac{40}{4} = 10$

Each book costs $10.

Spectrum Critical Thinking for Math
Grade 8
26

Lesson 3.4
Finding Slope Linear Relationships

Page 27

NAME _____

Lesson 3.5 Graphing a Line

The slope of a line represents the rate of change. The y–intercept is the point where the graph crosses the y–axis.

Graph and write the equation of the line that goes though the points (–3, 2) and (3, –6). Use the graph of the points to determine the slope. Use the line connecting the points to determine the y–intercept. What point with an x–coordinate of –9 would lie on the line?

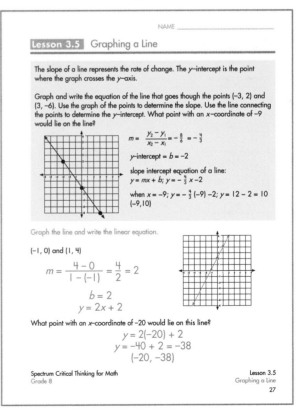

$m = \frac{y_2 - y_1}{x_2 - x_1} = -\frac{8}{6} = -\frac{4}{3}$

y–intercept = b = –2

slope intercept equation of a line:
$y = mx + b; \quad y = -\frac{4}{3}x - 2$

when $x = -9; y = -\frac{4}{3}(-9) - 2; y = 12 - 2 = 10$
(–9, 10)

Graph the line and write the linear equation.

(–1, 0) and (1, 4)

$m = \frac{4 - 0}{1 - (-1)} = \frac{4}{2} = 2$

$b = 2$
$y = 2x + 2$

What point with an x–coordinate of –20 would lie on this line?

$y = 2(-20) + 2$
$y = -40 + 2 = -38$
(–20, –38)

Spectrum Critical Thinking for Math
Grade 8

Lesson 3.5
Graphing a Line
27

Answer Key

Page 28

NAME _____

Lesson 3.5 Graphing a Line

Graph the lines and write the linear equation.

(–4, –3) and (0, 2)

What point with an x–coordinate of 14 would lie on this line?

$m = \dfrac{2 - (-3)}{0 - (-4)} = \dfrac{5}{4}$

$b = 2$

$y = \dfrac{5}{4}x + 2$

$y = \dfrac{5}{4}(14) + 2$

$y = \dfrac{39}{2}$; $(14, \dfrac{39}{2})$

(3, –3) and (–4, 4)

What point with a y–coordinate of –25 would lie on this line?

$m = \dfrac{4 - (-3)}{-4 - 3} = \dfrac{7}{-7} = -1$

$b = 0$

$y = -x$

$\dfrac{-25}{-1} = \dfrac{-x}{-1}$

$25 = x$

$(25, -25)$

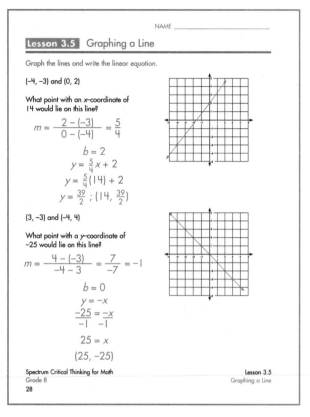

Spectrum Critical Thinking for Math
Grade 8
28

Lesson 3.5
Graphing a Line

Page 29

NAME _____

Lesson 3.6 Writing Linear Equations

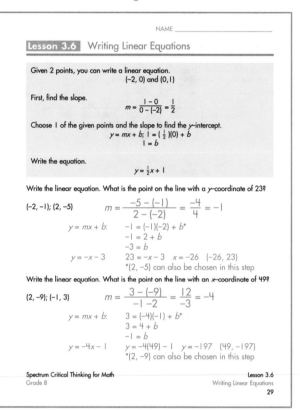

Given 2 points, you can write a linear equation.
(–2, 0) and (0,1)

First, find the slope.

$m = \dfrac{1 - 0}{0 - (-2)} = \dfrac{1}{2}$

Choose 1 of the given points and the slope to find the y–intercept.

$y = mx + b;\ 1 = (\dfrac{1}{2})(0) + b$
$1 = b$

Write the equation.

$y = \dfrac{1}{2}x + 1$

Write the linear equation. What is the point on the line with a y–coordinate of 23?

(–2, –1); (2, –5) $m = \dfrac{-5 - (-1)}{2 - (-2)} = \dfrac{-4}{4} = -1$

$y = mx + b:\quad -1 = (-1)(-2) + b^*$
$\qquad\qquad\qquad -1 = 2 + b$
$\qquad\qquad\qquad -3 = b$
$y = -x - 3\qquad 23 = -x - 3\quad x = -26\quad (-26, 23)$
$\qquad\qquad$ *(2, –5) can also be chosen in this step

Write the linear equation. What is the point on the line with an x–coordinate of 49?

(2, –9); (–1, 3) $m = \dfrac{3 - (-9)}{-1 - 2} = \dfrac{12}{-3} = -4$

$y = mx + b:\quad 3 = (-4)(-1) + b^*$
$\qquad\qquad\qquad 3 = 4 + b$
$\qquad\qquad\qquad -1 = b$
$y = -4x - 1\quad y = -4(49) - 1\quad y = -197\quad (49, -197)$
$\qquad\qquad$ *(2, –9) can also be chosen in this step

Spectrum Critical Thinking for Math
Grade 8

Lesson 3.6
Writing Linear Equations
29

Page 30

NAME _____

Lesson 3.7 Linear Systems of Equations

A set of two or more equations that contain two or more of the same variables is a system of equations.

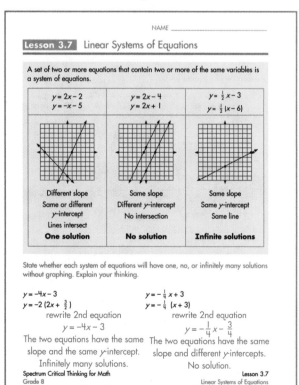

$y = 2x - 2$ $y = -x - 5$	$y = 2x - 4$ $y = 2x + 1$	$y = \dfrac{1}{2}x - 3$ $y = \dfrac{1}{2}(x - 6)$
Different slope Same or different y–intercept Lines intersect **One solution**	Same slope Different y–intercept No intersection **No solution**	Same slope Same y–intercept Same line **Infinite solutions**

State whether each system of equations will have one, no, or infinitely many solutions without graphing. Explain your thinking.

$y = -4x - 3$
$y = -2(2x + \dfrac{3}{2})$
$\quad$ rewrite 2nd equation
$\quad y = -4x - 3$
The two equations have the same slope and the same y–intercept.
Infinitely many solutions.

$y = -\dfrac{1}{4}x + 3$
$y = -\dfrac{1}{4}(x + 3)$
$\quad$ rewrite 2nd equation
$\quad y = -\dfrac{1}{4}x - \dfrac{3}{4}$
The two equations have the same slope and different y–intercepts.
No solution.

Spectrum Critical Thinking for Math
Grade 8
30

Lesson 3.7
Linear Systems of Equations

Page 31

NAME _____

Lesson 3.7 Linear Systems of Equations

An ordered pair that satisfies both equations in a system of equations is considered a solution.

Does (2,1) satisfy this system of equations? $\begin{cases} y = 6x - 11 \\ -4x - 6y = -14 \end{cases}$

Substitute the x and y into each equation to see if it is true:

$\begin{aligned} 1 &= 6(2) - 11 \\ 1 &= 12 - 11 \\ 1 &= 1 \\ \textbf{True} \end{aligned}$
$\qquad$
$\begin{aligned} -4(2) - 6(1) &= -14 \\ -8 - 6 &= -14 \\ -14 &= -14 \\ \textbf{True} \end{aligned}$

The ordered pair satisfies **both** equations, so it is a solution.

Show whether each ordered pair is a solution to the system of equations.

(0,–2)

$-\dfrac{1}{2}x + 3y = -6$
$-5x + y = -2$

$\begin{aligned} -\dfrac{1}{2}(0) + 3(-2) &= -6 \\ 0 + (-6) &= -6 \\ -6 &= -6 \\ \text{True} \end{aligned}$
$\qquad$
$\begin{aligned} -5(0) + (-2) &= -2 \\ 0 + (-2) &= -2 \\ -2 &= -2 \\ \text{True} \end{aligned}$

The ordered pair satisfies both equations, so it is a solution.

(2, –3)

$3x + 2y = 12$
$y = 5x - 7$

$\begin{aligned} 3(2) + 2(-3) &= 12 \\ 6 + (-6) &= 12 \\ 0 &= 12 \\ \text{False} \end{aligned}$
$\qquad$
$\begin{aligned} -3 &= 5(2) + 7 \\ 3 &= 10 - 7 \\ -3 &= 3 \\ \text{False} \end{aligned}$

The ordered pair does not satisfy both equations, so it is not a solution.

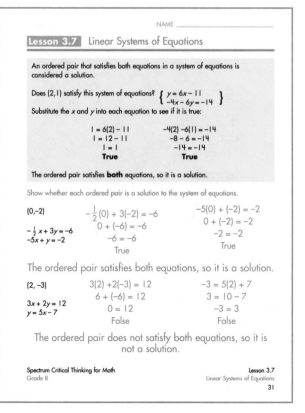

Spectrum Critical Thinking for Math
Grade 8

Lesson 3.7
Linear Systems of Equations
31

108

Page 32

NAME _____

Lesson 3.8 Linear Systems in the Real World

Tracy has $20 in her bank account and saves $10 each week. Eric has $50 in his account and saves $5 each week. When will they have the same amount of money? How much money will they have then?

Tracy: $y = 20 + 10x$; Eric: $y = 50 + 5x$

Replace y in one equation with the value of y in the other equation.

$20 + 10x = 50 + 5x$
$\underline{\quad -5x \quad -5x}$
$20 + 5x = 50$
$\underline{-20 \quad\quad -20}$
$5x = 30$

$\dfrac{5x}{5} = \dfrac{30}{5}$
$x = 6$

They will have the same amount of money after 6 weeks.

$y = 20 + 10(6) = 20 + 60 = 80$

They will have $80 at 6 weeks.

Solve the problems. Show your work.

The length of a rectangle is 6 times the width. The perimeter is 84 meters. What is the length and the width? What is the area of the rectangle?

$l = 6w$
$2l + 2w = 84$
$2(6w) + 2w = 84$
$12w + 2w = 84$
$14w = 84$

$w = 6m$
$l = 6(6)$
$l = 36m$
$A = lw$
$A = (36)(6) = 216m^2$

Tristan and Luke hiked a total of 18 miles in one weekend. Tristan hiked 6 miles more than Luke. How far did each person hike?

$t = 6 + l$
$t + l = 18;\ (6 + l) + l = 18$
$6 + 2l = 18$

$2l = 12$
$l = 6$ miles
$t = 6 + 6 = 12$ miles

Tristan hiked 12 miles. Luke hiked 6 miles.

Page 33

NAME _____

Lesson 3.8 Linear Systems in the Real World

Solve the problems. Show your work.

The sum of two numbers is 46. The second number is 4 less than the first. What are the two numbers?

$x + y = 46$
$y = x - 4$
$x + (x - 4) = 46$
$2x - 4 = 46$
$\underline{\quad +4 \quad +4}$

$2x = 50$
$\dfrac{2x}{2} = \dfrac{50}{2}$
$x = 25$
$y = 25 - 4;\ y = 21$

The two numbers are 25 and 21.

Hamilton and Liam are saving money. Hamilton started with $10 and deposits $5 a week. Liam started with $5 and saves $5 a week. When will they have the same amount of money?

Hamilton: $s = 10 + 5w$;
Liam: $s = 5 + 5w$

$10 + 5w = 5 + 5w$
$\underline{\quad -5w \quad -5w}$
$10 = 5$

They will never have the same amount of money.

No Solution

Valeria and Aiden are saving money. Valeria started with $10 and deposits $4 each week. Aiden started with $10 and makes two deposits of $2 each week. When will they have the same amount of money?

Valeria: $s = 10 + 4w$;
Aiden: $s = 10 + 2(2w) = 10 + 4w$

$10 + 4w = 10 + 4w$
$\underline{\quad -4w \quad -4w}$
$10 = 10$

They will have the same amount of money at the end of each week.

Page 34

NAME _____

💡 **Check What You Learned**

Linear Equations

1. Joey is training for a 5k race. She runs the same distance two days in a row. On the first day, she runs 5 laps around the track, and then runs an additional 1.5 miles. The next days she runs 3 laps, and an additional 4 miles. How long is each lap around the track?

Day 1: $d = 5l + 1.5$;
Day 2: $d = 3l + 4$

$5l + 1.5 = 3l + 4$
$\underline{-3l \quad\quad -3l}$
$2l + 1.5 = 4$
$\underline{\quad -1.5 \quad -1.5}$
$\dfrac{2l}{2} = \dfrac{2.5}{2}$
$l = 1.25$

Each lap is 1.25 miles.

2. Solve:
$-4(3a + 3) + 14 = -12a - 9$
$-12a - 12 + 14 = -12a - 9$
$-12a + 2 = -12a - 9$
$\underline{+12a \quad\quad +12a}$
$2 = -9$
No solution

3. Solve:
$3(6m - 4) + 8 = 2(9m - 2)$
$18m - 12 + 8 = 18m - 4$
$18m - 4 = 18m - 4$
$\underline{-18m \quad\quad -18m}$
$-4 = -4$
Infinitely many solutions

4. Find the rate of change for the table. Explain what the rate of change represents.

	27	13.5	67.5
Miles Driven	27	54	67.5	135
Gallons of Gas Remaining	14	13	12.5	10
	−1	−0.5	−2.5	

$\dfrac{27}{-1} = \dfrac{13.5}{-0.5} = \dfrac{67.5}{-2.5}$

$-\dfrac{27 \text{ miles}}{1 \text{ hour}}$

As the miles driven increase by 27 miles, the time to destination decreases by an hour.

CHAPTER 3 POSTTEST

Page 35

NAME _____

💡 **Check What You Learned**

Linear Equations

5. Find and interpret the slope:

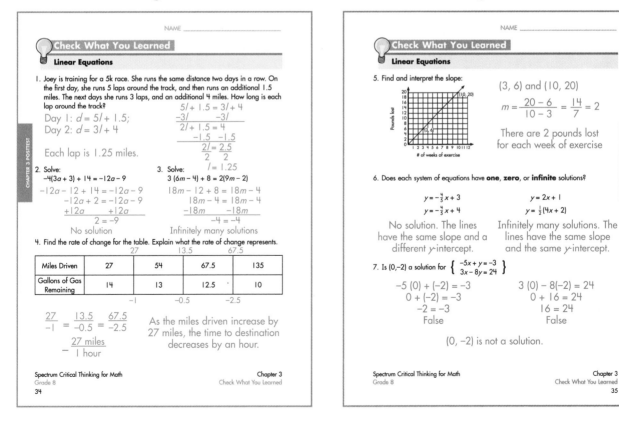

(3, 6) and (10, 20)

$m = \dfrac{20 - 6}{10 - 3} = \dfrac{14}{7} = 2$

There are 2 pounds lost for each week of exercise

6. Does each system of equations have **one, zero,** or **infinite** solutions?

$y = -\frac{4}{3}x + 3$
$y = -\frac{4}{3}x + 4$

No solution. The lines have the same slope and a different y-intercept.

$y = 2x + 1$
$y = \frac{1}{2}(4x + 2)$

Infinitely many solutions. The lines have the same slope and the same y-intercept.

7. Is (0,−2) a solution for $\left\{ \begin{array}{l} -5x + y = -3 \\ 3x - 8y = 24 \end{array} \right\}$

$-5(0) + (-2) = -3$
$0 + (-2) = -3$
$-2 = -3$
False

$3(0) - 8(-2) = 24$
$0 + 16 = 24$
$16 = 24$
False

(0, −2) is not a solution.

CHAPTER 3 POSTTEST

Answer Key

Page 36

Mid-Test Chapters 1–3

1. Find and explain the error in this calculation: $4^2 \cdot 4^6 = 4^{12}$

The exponents should have been added, not multiplied. The correct answer is 4^8.

2. Find and explain the error in this calculation: $\frac{5^{45}}{5^{17}} = 5^3$

The exponents should have been subtracted instead of divided. The correct answer is 5^{30}.

3. On average, there are 2.5×10^{13} red blood cells in the human body. There are 7×10^4 white blood cells. What is the ratio of red blood cells to white blood cells?

$$\frac{2.5 \times 10^{13}}{7 \times 10^4} = \frac{2.5}{7} \times \frac{10^{13}}{10^4} = 0.357 \times 10^9 = 3.57 \times 10^8$$

4. Human hair has an average diameter of 2.54×10^{-3}cm. If lighter hair has a diameter of 1.81×10^{-4}cm, what is the difference in diameter?

$2.54 \times 10^{-3} = 25.4 \times 10^{-4}$

$$\begin{array}{r} 25.4 \times 10^{-4} \\ -\ 1.81 \times 10^{-4} \\ \hline 23.59 \times 10^{-4} = \end{array}$$

2.359×10^{-3} cm

Page 37

Mid-Test Chapters 1–3

5. Is $\sqrt{\frac{81}{16}}$ rational or irrational? Explain your reasoning.

This is a rational number because it can be expressed as a fraction.

$$\sqrt{\frac{81}{16}} = \frac{\sqrt{81}}{\sqrt{16}} = \frac{9}{4}$$

6. Estimate the value of $\sqrt{175}$ to the nearest hundredth.

$\sqrt{169} < \sqrt{175} < \sqrt{196}$

$13 < \sqrt{175} < 14$

$175 - 169 = 6$

$196 - 169 = 27$

$\frac{6}{27} = 0.22$

$13 + 0.22 = 13.22$

7. A cube has a volume of 220 cubic centimeters. What is the approximate length of each side?

$V = s^3$

$220 = s^3$

$\sqrt[3]{220} = \sqrt[3]{s^3}$

$s = \sqrt[3]{220}$

$\sqrt[3]{216} < \sqrt[3]{220} < \sqrt[3]{343}$

$6 < \sqrt[3]{200} < 7$

$220 - 216 = 4$

$343 - 216 = 127$

$\frac{4}{127} = 0.03$

$6 + 0.03 = 6.03$

Each side is about 6.03 cm.

8. Put the numbers in order from least to greatest.

$-\frac{1}{3}, -\sqrt{3}, 3.3, \sqrt{9}, \frac{\sqrt{30}}{10}$

$$-\sqrt{3}, -\frac{1}{3}, \frac{\sqrt{30}}{10}, \sqrt{9}, 3.3$$

Page 38

Mid-Test Chapters 1–3

9. Solve: $6(x + 3) - 10 = 2(3x + 4)$

$$\begin{array}{c} 6x + 18 - 10 = 6x + 8 \\ 6x + 8 = 6x + 8 \\ \underline{-6x \qquad -6x} \\ 8 = 8 \end{array}$$

True. There are an infinite number of solutions.

10. Use the table to find the slope. What proportional relationship does the slope represent?

Number of Squats	5	10	15	20
Number of Bicep Curls	10	20	30	40

Using points (5, 10) and (10, 20)

$m = \frac{20 - 10}{10 - 5} = \frac{10}{5} = 2$

The slope is 2. There are 2 bicep curls for every squat.

11. iOrange Music Service charges $4.95 for 5 songs and $19.80 for 20 songs. What is the cost per song? Is there a flat fee to subscribe to the service?

(5, 4.95) and (20, 19.80)

$m = \frac{19.80 - 4.95}{20 - 5} = \frac{14.85}{15} = .99$

$$\begin{array}{c} 4.95 = 0.99(5) + b \\ 4.95 = 4.95 + b \\ \underline{-4.95 \quad -4.95} \\ b = 0 \end{array}$$

The cost per song is $0.99. There is no subscription fee.

Page 39

Mid-Test Chapters 1–3

12. There are 356 eighth-grade students at Euclid Middle School. 34 more than 4 times the number of girls is equal to half the number of boys. How many boys and girls are there at the school?

$g + b = 356$

$4g + 34 = 0.5b \rightarrow 8g + 68 = b$

$g + 8g + 68 = 356$

$9g + 68 = 356$

$\underline{-68 \quad -68}$

$9g = 288$

$\frac{9g}{9} = \frac{288}{9}$

$g = 32$

$32 + b = 356; b = 324$

There are 324 boys and 32 girls at the school.

13. Solve by graphing.

$\left\{ \begin{array}{l} y = \frac{1}{4}x - 4 \\ y = \frac{1}{4}x + 4 \end{array} \right\}$

The lines have the same slope and different y-intercepts. There is no solution.

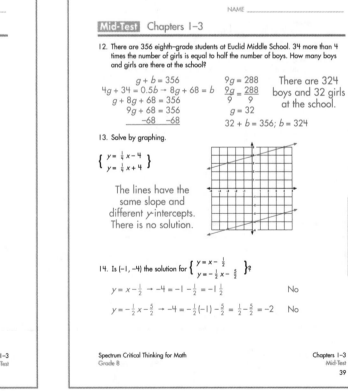

14. Is (−1, −4) the solution for $\left\{ \begin{array}{l} y = x - \frac{1}{2} \\ y = -\frac{1}{2}x - \frac{5}{2} \end{array} \right\}$?

$y = x - \frac{1}{2} \rightarrow -4 = -1 - \frac{1}{2} = -1\frac{1}{2}$ No

$y = -\frac{1}{2}x - \frac{5}{2} \rightarrow -4 = -\frac{1}{2}(-1) - \frac{5}{2} = \frac{1}{2} - \frac{5}{2} = -2$ No

Page 40

NAME _____

🔍 **Check What You Know**

Functions

1. State whether the table shows a function.

x	y
1	-4
2	-5
3	-6
4	-7
2	4

This is not a function. The x-value 2 does not have a unique y-value.

2. What can be added or taken away from the table in problem #1 to make it a function?

Either (2, 4) or (2, -5) should be removed in order to make the table a function.

Use the table to answer questions #3 – #6.

3. What is the rate of change in the table?

$$m = \frac{-5 - (-4)}{2 - 1} = -\frac{1}{1} = -1$$

x	y
1	-4
2	-5
3	-6
4	-7

4. What is the initial value of this function?

$y = mx + b$ $-4 = -1 + b$
$-4 = (-1)(1) + b$ $\underline{+1 \quad +1}$ The initial value is -3.
$-4 = -1 + b$ $-3 = b$

5. Write a linear equation for this table.

$y = -1x - 3$
$y = -x - 3$

Page 41

NAME _____

🔍 **Check What You Know**

Functions

6. Make a graph of the function on page 40.

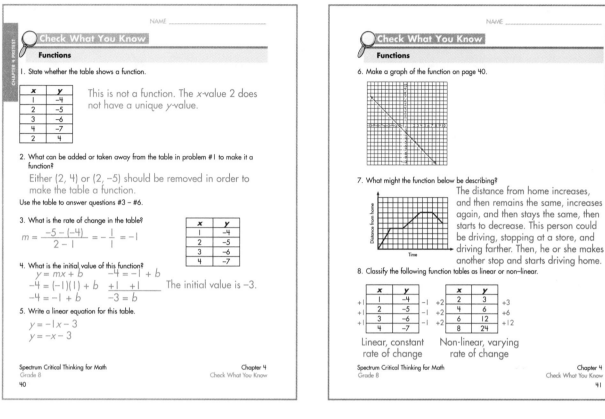

7. What might the function below be describing?

The distance from home increases, and then remains the same, increases again, and then stays the same, then starts to decrease. This person could be driving, stopping at a store, and driving farther. Then, he or she makes another stop and starts driving home.

8. Classify the following function tables as linear or non-linear.

x	y	
1	-4	
2	-5	
3	-6	
4	-7	

(+1 on x, -1 on y)

x	y	
2	3	+3
4	6	+6
6	12	+12
8	24	

Linear, constant rate of change   Non-linear, varying rate of change

Page 42

NAME _____

Lesson 4.1 Defining Functions

A function is a relationship where each input (independent variable) has exactly one output (dependent variable).

Is the relationship between a student's ID number and his or her name a function?

It is a function. Only one student is assigned to each ID number.

Is the relationship between the first and last names of students at a school a function?

It is not a function. Some students could have the same first name, but a different last name.

State whether each relationship is a function or not a function. Explain your answer.

The number of students and a teacher's 1st period class.
Not a function. There could be multiple classes with the same number of students.

The number of charms on a bracelet and the cost of the bracelet if the empty bracelet costs $30 and each charm added to the bracelet costs $12.
Function. The cost of the bracelet is unique to the number of charms on the bracelet. A bracelet with 2 charms will always have the same price.

A city and the state it is in.
Not a function. There could be cities with the same name in multiple states.

The amount of time that you study and your test grade.
Not a function. Two different students could study the same amount of time and get different test scores.

The length of the side of a square and the area of that square.
Function. The area will always be the square of the length of the side.

Page 43

NAME _____

Lesson 4.2 Function Tables

You can create a table of values using a function.

Chanel earns $12 an hour at her job, plus a weekly laundry supplement of $15 to dry clean her uniform. Her weekly pay is represented by the function $y = 12x + 15$. She doesn't work the same number of hours each week. Create a table of values to represent her weekly pay for a variety of hours worked.

Hours Worked	y = 12x + 15	Weekly Pay
5	$y = 12(5) + 15 = 60 + 15$	$75
10	$y = 12(10) + 15 = 120 + 15$	$135
15	$y = 12(15) + 15 = 180 + 15$	$195
20	$y = 12(20) + 15 = 240 + 15$	$255

Create a table of values for each function.

The UText cell phone company charges a $40 access fee plus $10 per gigabyte of data used.

GB Used	y = 10x + 40	Total Bill
5	$y = 10(5) + 40 = 50 + 40$	$90
10	$y = 10(10) + 40 = 100 + 40$	$140
15	$y = 10(15) + 40 = 150 + 40$	$190
20	$y = 10(20) + 40 = 200 + 40$	$240

A plumber charges a $50 house call fee plus $35 an hour for plumbing repairs.

GB Used	y = 35x + 50	Total Bill
5	$y = 35(5) + 50 = 175 + 50$	$225
10	$y = 35(10) + 50 = 350 + 50$	$400
15	$y = 35(15) + 50 = 525 + 50$	$575
20	$y = 35(20) + 50 = 700 + 50$	$750

Page 44

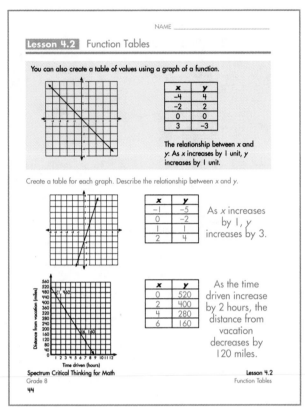

NAME _____

Lesson 4.2 Function Tables

You can also create a table of values using a graph of a function.

x	y
−4	4
−2	2
0	0
3	−3

The relationship between x and y: As x increases by 1 unit, y increases by 1 unit.

Create a table for each graph. Describe the relationship between x and y.

x	y
−1	−5
0	−2
1	1
2	4

As x increases by 1, y increases by 3.

x	y
0	520
2	400
4	280
6	160

As the time driven increase by 2 hours, the distance from vacation decreases by 120 miles.

Spectrum Critical Thinking for Math
Grade 8
44

Lesson 4.2
Function Tables

Page 45

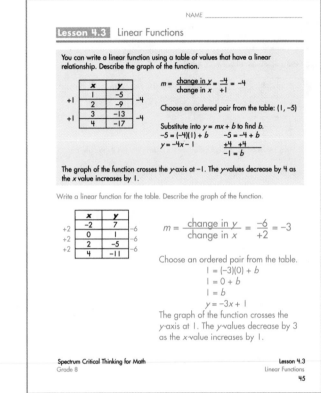

NAME _____

Lesson 4.3 Linear Functions

You can write a linear function using a table of values that have a linear relationship. Describe the graph of the function.

x	y
1	−5
2	−9
3	−13
4	−17

$m = \dfrac{\text{change in } y}{\text{change in } x} = \dfrac{-4}{+1} = -4$

Choose an ordered pair from the table: (1, −5)

Substitute into $y = mx + b$ to find b.
$-5 = (-4)(1) + b$ $-5 = -4 + b$
$y = -4x - 1$ $\dfrac{+4 \quad +4}{-1 = b}$

The graph of the function crosses the y-axis at −1. The y-values decrease by 4 as the x value increases by 1.

Write a linear function for the table. Describe the graph of the function.

x	y
−2	7
0	1
2	−5
4	−11

$m = \dfrac{\text{change in } y}{\text{change in } x} = \dfrac{-6}{+2} = -3$

Choose an ordered pair from the table.
$1 = (-3)(0) + b$
$1 = 0 + b$
$1 = b$
$y = -3x + 1$
The graph of the function crosses the y-axis at 1. The y-values decrease by 3 as the x-value increases by 1.

Spectrum Critical Thinking for Math
Grade 8

Lesson 4.3
Linear Functions
45

Page 46

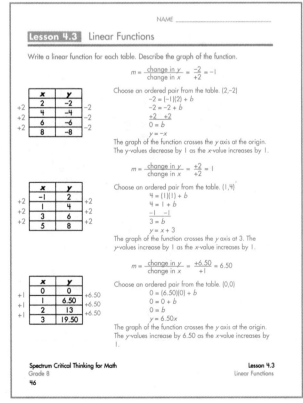

NAME _____

Lesson 4.3 Linear Functions

Write a linear function for each table. Describe the graph of the function.

$m = \dfrac{\text{change in } y}{\text{change in } x} = \dfrac{-2}{+2} = -1$

x	y
2	−2
4	−4
6	−6
8	−8

Choose an ordered pair from the table. (2,−2)
$-2 = (-1)(2) + b$
$-2 = -2 + b$
$\dfrac{+2 \quad +2}{0 = b}$
$y = -x$
The graph of the function crosses the y axis at the origin. The y-values decrease by 1 as the x-value increases by 1.

$m = \dfrac{\text{change in } y}{\text{change in } x} = \dfrac{+2}{+2} = 1$

x	y
−1	2
1	4
3	6
5	8

Choose an ordered pair from the table. (1,4)
$4 = (1)(1) + b$
$4 = 1 + b$
$\dfrac{-1 \quad -1}{3 = b}$
$y = x + 3$
The graph of the function crosses the y axis at 3. The y-values increase by 1 as the x-value increases by 1.

$m = \dfrac{\text{change in } y}{\text{change in } x} = \dfrac{+6.50}{+1} = 6.50$

x	y
0	0
1	6.50
2	13
3	19.50

Choose an ordered pair from the table. (0,0)
$0 = (6.50)(0) + b$
$0 = 0 + b$
$0 = b$
$y = 6.50x$
The graph of the function crosses the y axis at the origin. The y-values increase by 6.50 as the x-value increases by 1.

Spectrum Critical Thinking for Math
Grade 8
46

Lesson 4.3
Linear Functions

Page 47

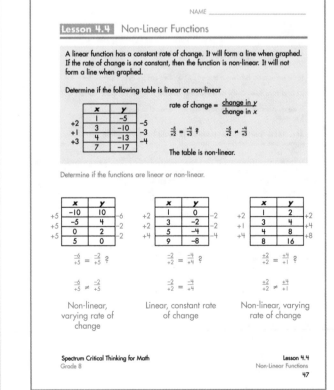

NAME _____

Lesson 4.4 Non-Linear Functions

A linear function has a constant rate of change. It will form a line when graphed. If the rate of change is not constant, then the function is non-linear. It will not form a line when graphed.

Determine if the following table is linear or non-linear.

x	y
1	−5
3	−10
4	−13
7	−17

rate of change $= \dfrac{\text{change in } y}{\text{change in } x}$

$\dfrac{-5}{+2} = \dfrac{-3}{+1}$? $\dfrac{-5}{+2} \neq \dfrac{-3}{+1}$

The table is non-linear.

Determine if the functions are linear or non-linear.

x	y
−10	10
−5	4
0	2
5	0

$\dfrac{-6}{+5} = \dfrac{-2}{+5}$?

$\dfrac{-6}{+5} \neq \dfrac{-2}{+5}$

Non-linear, varying rate of change

x	y
1	0
3	−2
5	−4
9	−8

$\dfrac{-2}{+2} = \dfrac{-4}{+4}$?

$\dfrac{-2}{+2} = \dfrac{-4}{+4}$

Linear, constant rate of change

x	y
1	2
3	4
4	8
8	16

$\dfrac{+2}{+2} = \dfrac{+4}{+1}$?

$\dfrac{+2}{+2} \neq \dfrac{+4}{+1}$

Non-linear, varying rate of change

Spectrum Critical Thinking for Math
Grade 8

Lesson 4.4
Non-Linear Functions
47

Page 48

Lesson 4.4 Non-Linear Functions

If a description of a function indicates that the rate of change is constant, then it describes a linear function.

Hats R Us creates custom hats. It charges $7.50 for the hat and $0.75 for each letter that is stitched on the hat.

Linear. The cost of the hat increases by $0.75 for each letter that is stitched onto the hat.

The area of a square is the square of the length of one side of the square.

Non-linear. The area of a square doesn't increase by a constant amount as the length of the side increases. For example, the difference in area from a 1cm square to a 2cm square is 3cm², but the difference from a 2cm square to a 3cm square is 5cm².

Determine if each function is linear or non-linear.

The distance of the minute hand from the 12 on a clock as the minute hand moves around the clock.
Non-linear. The distance from the 12 increases, until the minute hand passes the 6, and then the distance starts to decrease.

The amount of protein in the can as Vince uses one scoop of protein power each day in his smoothie.

Linear. The amount of powder in the can decreases by 1 scoop each day.

Parking fees if $2.00 is charged for the first hour, $1.00 is charged per hour for the 2nd through the 5th hour, and a flat fee of $5 is charged for more than 7 hours.
Non-linear. The cost does not increase by the same amount as the amount of time increases.

The number of bacteria being grown in a lab, if their number doubles every 2 hours.
Non-linear. The increase in the number of bacteria is different every two hours.

Page 49

Lesson 4.5 Rate of Change

Slope and rate of change are the same thing. Rate of change can be found using a table, graph, or equation. It can also be found using a written description.

Jessica has a t-shirt printing business. She charges a $30 design fee and $4 per t-shirt. What is the rate of change?

The cost increases by $4 for every t-shirt that is ordered.

Answer the questions.

After walking a mile, Vanessa starts jogging at a speed of 7 miles per hour. What is her rate of change each hour after she starts jogging?

$$\frac{7 \text{ miles}}{1 \text{ hour}} = 7 \frac{\text{miles}}{\text{hour}}$$

Rebecca puts 10 gallons of gas in her car. She uses $1\frac{1}{4}$ gallons of gas for every 30 minutes that she drives. What is her rate of change for each hour?

$$\frac{1.25 \text{ gallons}}{0.5 \text{ hours}} = 2.50 \frac{\text{gallons}}{\text{hour}}$$

At the basketball game, there are 50 students in the stands watching the game. 3 more students enter the stands every 2 minutes. What is the rate of change in the number of people entering the gym to watch the game?

$$\frac{3 \text{ students}}{2 \text{ minutes}} = 1.5 \frac{\text{students}}{\text{minute}}$$

Page 50

Lesson 4.6 Initial Value

The y-intercept and initial value are the same thing. It can be calculated from a table, graph, or equation, or taken from a verbal description.

Jessica has a t-shirt printing business. She charges a $30 design fee and $4 per t-shirt. What is the initial value?

The initial cost of the t-shirts is $30 because Jessica will have to pay $30 no matter how many t-shirts she orders.

Find the initial value in each description.

Jennifer has 8 gallons of gas in her car. The amount of gas decreases by $1\frac{1}{3}$ gallons of gas for every 30 minutes that she drives.

initial value = 8 gallons

Maria borrowed $75 from her father to buy concert tickets. She pays him back $20 every 2 weeks.

initial value = $75

At the football game, 75 students are already in the stands watching the game, and 3 students the game every 2 minutes.

initial value = 75 students

Dawn is driving home from her aunt's house, which is 45 miles away from her home. She is 10 miles closer to home for every 15 minutes that pass.

initial value = 45 miles

Page 51

Lesson 4.7 Interpreting Functions

The meaning of a function can be interpreted by analyzing the rate of change and initial value of a function.

In the function $c = 25n + 20$, c is the cost of the cell phone bill, and n is the number of users on the phone plan. How much is charged for each user on the plan? What is the fee for having an account?

The cell phone bill is $25 per user on the plan, plus an account access fee of $20.

Answer the question about each function.

In the function $r = 2p + 50$, r is the number of rewards points at a video game store, and p is the amount of a store purchase. How many points does this customer already have?

The customer has 50 points already.
2 points can be earned for every dollar spent.

Rewrite the equation for a customer who had 75 rewards points before he or she made the purchase.

$$r = 2p + 75$$

In the function $s = 900 - 50w$, s is the amount in a savings account, and w is the number of weeks since school started. Jada worked all summer to save money that she could spend during the school year. How much does she spend each week?

Jada uses $50 a week.

How much did Jada save during the summer?

She saved $900.

Answer Key

Page 52

Lesson 4.7 Interpreting Functions

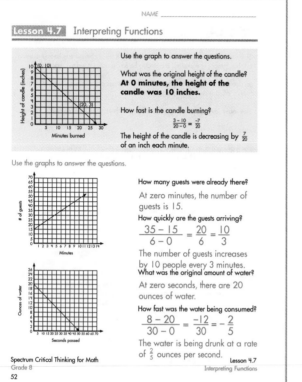

Use the graph to answer the questions.

What was the original height of the candle?
At 0 minutes, the height of the candle was 10 inches.

How fast is the candle burning?
$$\frac{3 - 10}{20 - 0} = \frac{-7}{20}$$
The height of the candle is decreasing by $\frac{7}{20}$ of an inch each minute.

Use the graphs to answer the questions.

How many guests were already there?
At zero minutes, the number of guests is 15.

How quickly are the guests arriving?
$$\frac{35 - 15}{6 - 0} = \frac{20}{6} = \frac{10}{3}$$
The number of guests increases by 10 people every 3 minutes.

What was the original amount of water?
At zero seconds, there are 20 ounces of water.

How fast was the water being consumed?
$$\frac{8 - 20}{30 - 0} = \frac{-12}{30} = -\frac{2}{5}$$
The water is being drunk at a rate of $\frac{2}{5}$ ounces per second.

Page 53

Lesson 4.8 Analyzing Functions

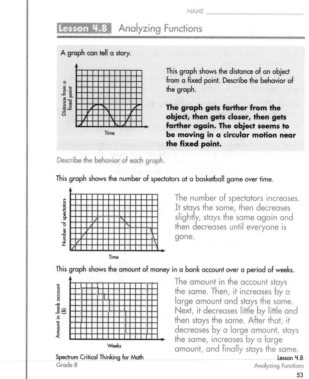

A graph can tell a story.

This graph shows the distance of an object from a fixed point. Describe the behavior of the graph.

The graph gets farther from the object, then gets closer, then gets farther again. The object seems to be moving in a circular motion near the fixed point.

Describe the behavior of each graph.

This graph shows the number of spectators at a basketball game over time.

The number of spectators increases. It stays the same, then decreases slightly, stays the same again and then decreases until everyone is gone.

This graph shows the amount of money in a bank account over a period of weeks.

The amount in the account stays the same. Then, it increases by a large amount and stays the same. Next, it decreases little by little and then stays the same. After that, it decreases by a large amount, stays the same, increases by a large amount, and finally stays the same.

Page 54

Lesson 4.9 Constructing Functions in the Real World

Write a linear equation to describe this relationship: 5°F = −15°C and −40°F = −40°C. Use it to find the Celsius temperature when the Fahrenheit temperature is 0°F and 60°F.

(5,−15) and (−40,−40) are the ordered pairs. $\frac{-40 - (-15)}{-40 - 5} = \frac{-25}{-45} = \frac{5}{9}$

$$y = mx + b$$
$$-15 = \frac{5}{9}(5) + b$$
$$-15 = \frac{25}{9} + b$$
$$\frac{-\frac{25}{9} \quad -\frac{25}{9}}{b = -\frac{160}{9}}$$
$$°C = \frac{5}{9}°F - \frac{160}{9}$$
$$°C = \frac{5}{9}(°F - 32)$$

$$0°F = ?°C$$
$$°C = \frac{5}{9}(0 - 32) = -17.78$$
$$0°F = -17.78°C$$

$$60°F = ?°C$$
$$°C = \frac{5}{9}(60 - 32) = 15.56$$
$$60°F = 15.56°C$$

Answer the question. Show your work.

Robert rents a van. He pays $105 when he drives 150 miles. Diane rents a van. She drives 100 miles and has to pay $80. Write an equation to represent the cost. What proportional relationship does the equation represent?

(150, 105) and (100, 80)

$$m = \frac{80 - 105}{100 - 150} = \frac{-25}{-50} = 0.5$$

$$80 = 0.5(100) + b$$
$$80 = 50 + b$$
$$\frac{-50 \quad -50}{30 = b}$$

The rental company charges $0.50 per mile with a flat fee of $30.

$$y = 0.5x + 30$$

Page 55

Lesson 4.9 Constructing Functions in the Real World

Answer the questions. Show your work.

DJ is training for a long-distance bike race. He starts recording his time and distance after he has already been riding for awhile. An hour later, he has traveled 24 miles and after 3 hours he has traveled 40 miles. Write an equation to describe the relationship.

(1, 24) and (3, 40)

$$m = \frac{40 - 24}{3 - 1} = \frac{16}{2} = 8 \text{ miles per hour}$$

$$y = mx + b$$
$$24 = 8(1) + b$$
$$24 = 8 + b$$
$$\frac{-8 \quad -8}{16 = b}$$
$$y = 8x + 16$$

What do the intercept and rate of change represent?

The y-intercept represents the number of miles already traveled.

The rate of change is the speed that he is biking.

The boiling point of water is 213°F at 500 feet below sea level and 207.5°F at 2,500 feet above sea level. What is the boiling point at sea level?

(−500, 213) and (2500, 207.5)

$$m = \frac{207.5 - 213}{2500 - (-500)} = \frac{-5.5}{3000} = -0.00183$$

$$y = mx + b$$
$$213 = -0.00183(-500) + b$$
$$213 = 0.915 + b$$
$$\frac{-0.915 \quad -0.915}{212.1 = b}$$

$$y = -0.00183x + 212.1$$
$$y = -0.00183(0) + 212.1$$
$$y = 212.1°F \text{ at sea level}$$

Answer Key

Page 56

NAME _____

Lesson 4.10 Comparing Functions

The table represents the balance on a loan that Jamie took out from her mother.

Time (weeks) since loan	Debt ($)
1	−80
3	−60
6	−30

Kenneth took a loan from his mother at the same time. The equation representing his debt is $y = 15x − 110$. Which person is paying their mother more money per week? Who took out the largest loan?

Jamie
$m = \frac{−60 − (−80)}{3 − 1} = \frac{20}{2} = \$10$
Jamie is paying $10 a week.
$y = mx + b$
$−30 = (10)(6) + b$
$−90 = b$
Jamie borrowed $90.

Kenneth
$m = 15$
Kenneth is paying $15 a week.
$b = −110$
Kenneth borrowed $110 from his mother.

Kenneth took out the largest loan and is paying back the most each week.

Tank A started with 9 feet of water and is being drained at 0.5 feet every 30 minutes. Tank B's drainage can be represented with the equation: $f = −0.75h + 10$, where f = feet of water and h = the number of hours that have passed. Which tank started with the most water? Which tank is draining faster?

Tank A
Rate of change = $\frac{−0.5 \text{ feet}}{0.5 \text{ hours}} = −1 \frac{\text{ft.}}{\text{hour}}$

Tank B
Rate of change = $−0.75 \frac{\text{ft.}}{\text{hour}}$

Initial height is 9 feet.

Initial height is 10 feet.

Tank B started with the most water and Tank A is draining faster.

Page 57

NAME _____

Lesson 4.10 Comparing Functions

Answer the questions. Show your work.

Who needs the most Service Learning Hours: Tammy or Timmy? Who is volunteering the most hours each week?

Service learning hours Tammy needs:

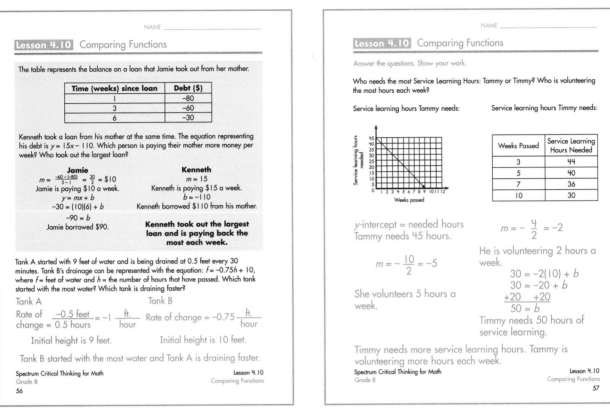

Service learning hours Timmy needs:

Weeks Passed	Service Learning Hours Needed
3	44
5	40
7	36
10	30

y-intercept = needed hours
Tammy needs 45 hours.

$m = −\frac{10}{2} = −5$

She volunteers 5 hours a week.

$m = −\frac{4}{2} = −2$

He is volunteering 2 hours a week.
$30 = −2(10) + b$
$30 = −20 + b$
$\underline{+20 \quad +20}$
$50 = b$

Timmy needs 50 hours of service learning.

Timmy needs more service learning hours. Tammy is volunteering more hours each week.

Page 58

NAME _____

Check What You Learned

Functions

Use the table to answer the questions.

Wholesale Cost	Retail Cost
$9.50	$19.40
$12.50	$23.00
$14.00	$24.80
$20.00	$32.00

1. What is the rate of change shown in this table?

$$m = \frac{23 − 19.40}{12.50 − 9.50} = \frac{3.6}{3} = 1.2$$

2. What is the initial value of this function?
$y = mx + b$
$23 = 1.2(12.50) + b$
$23 = 15 + b$
$\underline{−15 \quad −15}$
$8 = b$

3. Write a linear equation for the table.
$y = mx + b$
$m = 1.2; b = 8$
$y = 1.2x + 8$

Page 59

NAME _____

Check What You Learned

Functions

Use the table to answer questions 4 and 5.

4. What is the meaning of the rate of change and initial value for this table?

Wholesale Cost	Retail Cost
9.50	19.40
12.50	23.00
14.00	24.80
20.00	32.00

$y = 1.2x + 8$; retail cost is 20% more than wholesale cost, plus an $8 markup.

5. Make a graph of this function.

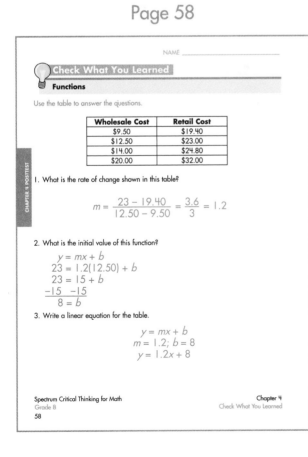

6. Zayn is filling a hole in the ground that is 30 inches deep. He is filling the hole at a rate of 3 inches in 15 minutes. The equation $h = −12x + 30$ represents the depth, h, of the hole after x hours. How long will it take for the hole to be half full?

$15 = −12x + 30$
$\underline{−30 \qquad −30}$
$−15 = −12x$
$\frac{−15}{−12} = \frac{−12x}{−12}$

$\frac{5}{4} = x$

It would take an hour and 15 minutes.

Answer Key

Page 60

NAME _____

Check What You Learned
Functions

7. This graph shows the speed of someone driving. What could be happening in the section of the graph where the speed is touching the *x*-axis?

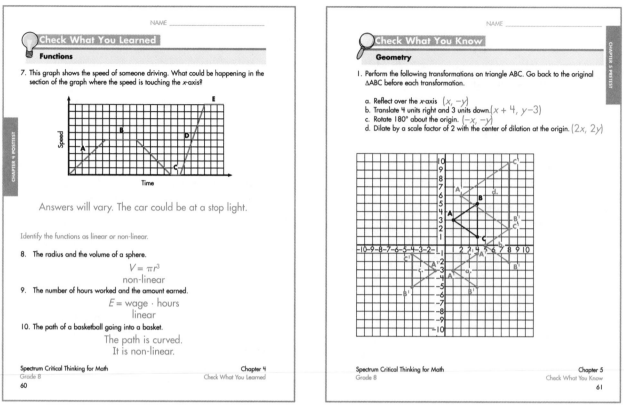

Answers will vary. The car could be at a stop light.

Identify the functions as linear or non-linear.

8. The radius and the volume of a sphere.
$$V = \pi r^3$$
non-linear

9. The number of hours worked and the amount earned.
$$E = \text{wage} \cdot \text{hours}$$
linear

10. The path of a basketball going into a basket.
The path is curved.
It is non-linear.

Page 61

NAME _____

Check What You Know
Geometry

1. Perform the following transformations on triangle ABC. Go back to the original ∆ABC before each transformation.

   a. Reflect over the *x*-axis $(x, -y)$
   b. Translate 4 units right and 3 units down. $(x + 4, y-3)$
   c. Rotate 180° about the origin. $(-x, -y)$
   d. Dilate by a scale factor of 2 with the center of dilation at the origin. $(2x, 2y)$

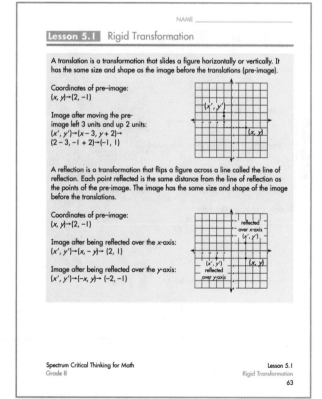

Page 62

NAME _____

Check What You Know
Geometry

2. What angle(s) are congruent to ∠7?

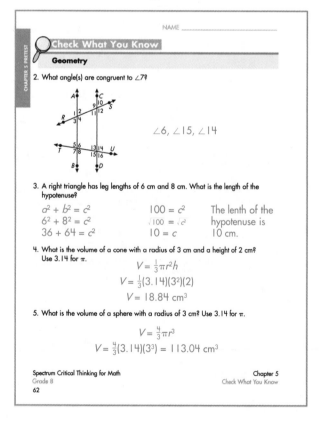

$$\angle 6, \angle 15, \angle 14$$

3. A right triangle has leg lengths of 6 cm and 8 cm. What is the length of the hypotenuse?

$$a^2 + b^2 = c^2 \qquad 100 = c^2 \qquad \text{The lenth of the}$$
$$6^2 + 8^2 = c^2 \qquad \sqrt{100} = \sqrt{c^2} \qquad \text{hypotenuse is}$$
$$36 + 64 = c^2 \qquad 10 = c \qquad 10 \text{ cm.}$$

4. What is the volume of a cone with a radius of 3 cm and a height of 2 cm? Use 3.14 for π.
$$V = \tfrac{1}{3}\pi r^2 h$$
$$V = \tfrac{1}{3}(3.14)(3^2)(2)$$
$$V = 18.84 \text{ cm}^3$$

5. What is the volume of a sphere with a radius of 3 cm? Use 3.14 for π.
$$V = \tfrac{4}{3}\pi r^3$$
$$V = \tfrac{4}{3}(3.14)(3^3) = 113.04 \text{ cm}^3$$

Page 63

NAME _____

Lesson 5.1 Rigid Transformation

A translation is a transformation that slides a figure horizontally or vertically. It has the same size and shape as the image before the translations (pre-image).

Coordinates of pre-image:
$(x, y) \rightarrow (2, -1)$

Image after moving the pre-image left 3 units and up 2 units:
$(x', y') \rightarrow (x - 3, y + 2) \rightarrow$
$(2 - 3, -1 + 2) \rightarrow (-1, 1)$

A reflection is a transformation that flips a figure across a line called the line of reflection. Each point reflected is the same distance from the line of reflection as the points of the pre-image. The image has the same size and shape of the image before the translations.

Coordinates of pre-image:
$(x, y) \rightarrow (2, -1)$

Image after being reflected over the *x*-axis:
$(x', y') \rightarrow (x, -y) \rightarrow (2, 1)$

Image after being reflected over the *y*-axis:
$(x', y') \rightarrow (-x, y) \rightarrow (-2, -1)$

Page 64

NAME _____

Lesson 5.1 Rigid Transformations

Video game designers use transformations to control the movement of game figures. Use the diagram of the game scene to answer the following questions. Show the transformations on the graph.

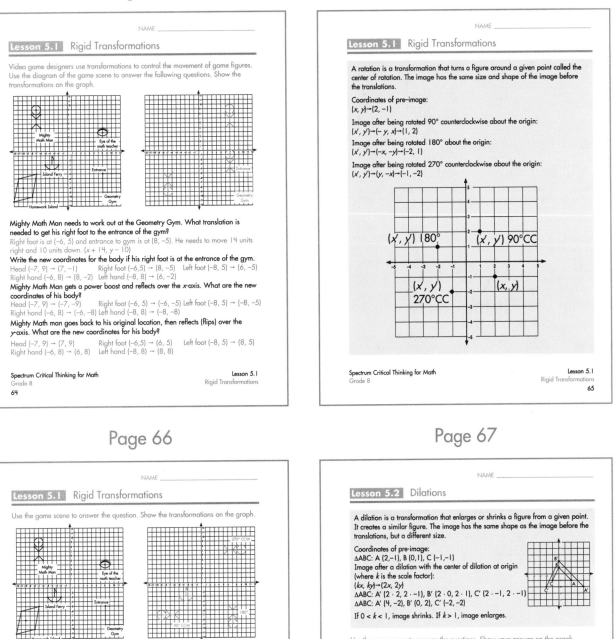

Mighty Math Man needs to work out at the Geometry Gym. What translation is needed to get his right foot to the entrance of the gym?

Right foot is at (–6, 5) and entrance to gym is at (8, –5). He needs to move 14 units right and 10 units down. (x + 14, y – 10)

Write the new coordinates for the body if his right foot is at the entrance of the gym.

Head (–7, 9) → (7, –1)   Right foot (–6,5) → (8, –5)   Left foot (–8, 5) → (6, –5)
Right hand (–6, 8) → (8, –2) Left hand (–8, 8) → (6, –2)

Mighty Math Man gets a power boost and reflects over the x-axis. What are the new coordinates of his body?

Head (–7, 9) → (–7, –9)   Right foot (–6, 5) → –6, –5) Left foot (–8, 5) → (–8, –5)
Right hand (–6, 8) → (–6, –8) Left hand (–8, 8) → (–8, –8)

Mighty Math man goes back to his original location, then reflects (flips) over the y-axis. What are the new coordinates for his body?

Head (–7, 9) → (7, 9)   Right foot (–6,5) → (6, 5)   Left foot (–8, 5) → (8, 5)
Right hand (–6, 8) → (6, 8) Left hand (–8, 8) → (8, 8)

Spectrum Critical Thinking for Math
Grade 8
64

Lesson 5.1
Rigid Transformations

Page 65

NAME _____

Lesson 5.1 Rigid Transformations

A rotation is a transformation that turns a figure around a given point called the center of rotation. The image has the same size and shape of the image before the translations.

Coordinates of pre-image:
(x, y)→(2, –1)

Image after being rotated 90° counterclockwise about the origin:
(x', y')→(– y, x)→(1, 2)

Image after being rotated 180° about the origin:
(x', y')→(–x, –y)→(–2, 1)

Image after being rotated 270° counterclockwise about the origin:
(x', y')→(y, –x)→(–1, –2)

Spectrum Critical Thinking for Math
Grade 8

Lesson 5.1
Rigid Transformations
65

Page 66

NAME _____

Lesson 5.1 Rigid Transformations

Use the game scene to answer the question. Show the transformations on the graph.

Mighty Math Man is having so much fun solving math problems that he spins around! Which rotation about the origin will get him closest to the Island Ferry: 90° CCW, 180°, or 270° CCW?

Ferry is between (–5, –3) → (–2, –3)

90° CCW (–y, x)
Head (–7, 9) → (–9, –7); Right hand (–6, 8) → (–8, –6); Left hand (–8, 8) → (–8, –8); Right foot (–6,5) → (–5, –6); Left foot (–8, 5) → (–5, –8)

180° CCW (–x, –y)
Head (–7, 9) → (7, –9); Right hand (–6, 8) → (6, –8); Left hand (–8, 8) → (8, –8); Right foot (–6,5) → (6, –5); Left foot (–8, 5) → (8, –5)

270° CCW (y, –x)
Head (–7, 9) → (9, 7); Right hand (–6, 8) → (8, 6); Left hand (–8, 8) → (8, 8); Right foot (–6,5) → (5, 6); Left foot (–8, 5) → (5, 8)

The 90° CCW rotation is the closest to the ferry.

Spectrum Critical Thinking for Math
Grade 8
66

Lesson 5.1
Rigid Transformations

Page 67

NAME _____

Lesson 5.2 Dilations

A dilation is a transformation that enlarges or shrinks a figure from a given point. It creates a similar figure. The image has the same shape as the image before the translations, but a different size.

Coordinates of pre-image:
△ABC: A (2,–1), B (0,1), C (–1,–1)
Image after a dilation with the center of dilation at origin (where k is the scale factor):
(kx, ky)→(2x, 2y)
△ABC: A' (2 · 2, 2 · –1), B' (2 · 0, 2 · 1), C' (2 · –1, 2 · –1)
△ABC: A' (4, –2), B' (0, 2), C' (–2, –2)

If 0 < k < 1, image shrinks. If k > 1, image enlarges.

Use the game scene to answer the questions. Show your answer on the graph.

The Eye of the Math Teacher gets bigger when Mighty Math Man gets a problem right. The eye needs to grow by 2 because Mighty Math Man just got three problems right. What are the new coordinates of the center and each corner of the eye?

New coordinates (2x, 2y) eye center (8, 4) → (16, 8); left corner (7, 4) → (14, 8); right corner (9, 4) → (18, 8)

Spectrum Critical Thinking for Math
Grade 8

Lesson 5.2
Dilations
67

Answer Key

Page 68

Lesson 5.2 Dilations

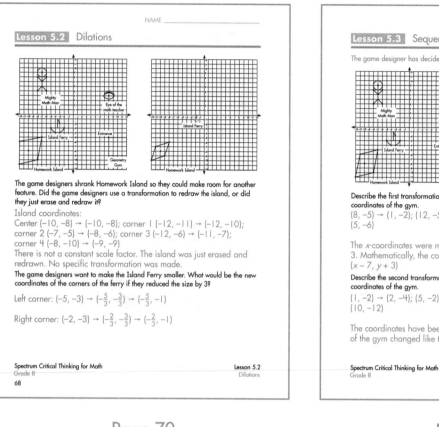

The game designers shrank Homework Island so they could make room for another feature. Did the game designers use a transformation to redraw the island, or did they just erase and redraw it?

Island coordinates:

Center (–10, –8) → (–10, –8); corner 1 (–12, –11) → (–12, –10); corner 2 (–7, –5) → (–8, –6); corner 3 (–12, –6) → (–11, –7); corner 4 (–8, –10) → (–9, –9)

There is not a constant scale factor. The island was just erased and redrawn. No specific transformation was made.

The game designers want to make the Island Ferry smaller. What would be the new coordinates of the corners of the ferry if they reduced the size by 3?

Left corner: $(-5, -3) \rightarrow (-\frac{5}{3}, -\frac{3}{3}) \rightarrow (-\frac{5}{3}, -1)$

Right corner: $(-2, -3) \rightarrow (-\frac{2}{3}, -\frac{3}{3}) \rightarrow (-\frac{2}{3}, -1)$

Page 69

Lesson 5.3 Sequence of Transformations

The game designer has decided to move the Geometry Gym and then make it larger.

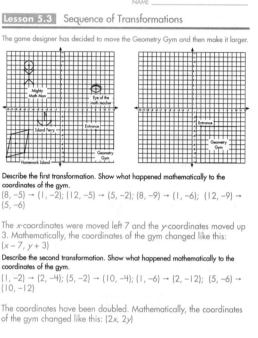

Describe the first transformation. Show what happened mathematically to the coordinates of the gym.

(8, –5) → (1, –2); (12, –5) → (5, –2); (8, –9) → (1, –6); (12, –9) → (5, –6)

The x-coordinates were moved left 7 and the y-coordinates moved up 3. Mathematically, the coordinates of the gym changed like this: (x – 7, y + 3)

Describe the second transformation. Show what happened mathematically to the coordinates of the gym.

(1, –2) → (2, –4); (5, –2) → (10, –4); (1, –6) → (2, –12); (5, –6) → (10, –12)

The coordinates have been doubled. Mathematically, the coordinates of the gym changed like this: (2x, 2y)

Page 70

Lesson 5.3 Sequence of Transformations

The game designer wants to put Homework Island on the first quadrant.

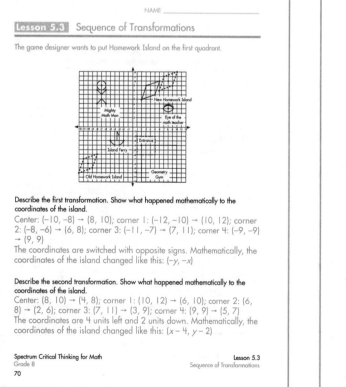

Describe the first transformation. Show what happened mathematically to the coordinates of the island.

Center: (–10, –8) → (8, 10); corner 1: (–12, –10) → (10, 12); corner 2: (–8, –6) → (6, 8); corner 3: (–11, –7) → (7, 11); corner 4: (–9, –9) → (9, 9)

The coordinates are switched with opposite signs. Mathematically, the coordinates of the island changed like this: (–y, –x)

Describe the second transformation. Show what happened mathematically to the coordinates of the island.

Center: (8, 10) → (4, 8); corner 1: (10, 12) → (6, 10); corner 2: (6, 8) → (2, 6); corner 3: (7, 11) → (3, 9); corner 4: (9, 9) → (5, 7)

The coordinates are 4 units left and 2 units down. Mathematically, the coordinates of the island changed like this: (x – 4, y – 2)

Page 71

Lesson 5.4 Slope and Similar Triangles

You can use similar triangles to explain why the slope is the same between any two distinct points on a non-vertical line in the coordinate plane. Follow the directions below to prove that the slope is the same between any two distinct points on a line.

Draw a right triangle with the hypotenuse being the line segment between the points (–8,8) and (–6,6). What is the ratio of the length of the vertical leg to the length of the horizontal leg?

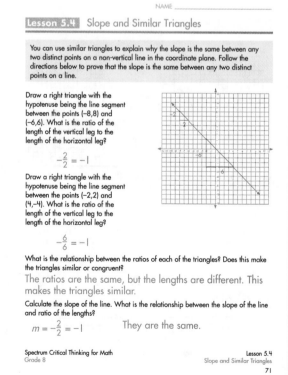

$-\frac{2}{2} = -1$

Draw a right triangle with the hypotenuse being the line segment between the points (–2,2) and (4,–4). What is the ratio of the length of the vertical leg to the length of the horizontal leg?

$-\frac{6}{6} = -1$

What is the relationship between the ratios of each of the triangles? Does this make the triangles similar or congruent?

The ratios are the same, but the lengths are different. This makes the triangles similar.

Calculate the slope of the line. What is the relationship between the slope of the line and ratio of the lengths?

$m = -\frac{2}{2} = -1$ They are the same.

Answer Key

Page 72

NAME _____

Lesson 5.5 Transversals and Calculating Angles

A transversal is a line that intersects two or more lines at different points. Angle pairs formed by the intersections are congruent. The angle pairs are:

Exterior

Interior

Exterior

Angle Pairs	Examples
Alternate interior angles	$\angle4, \angle5; \angle3, \angle6$
Alternate exterior angles	$\angle2, \angle7; \angle1, \angle8$
Corresponding angles	$\angle1, \angle5; \angle3, \angle7; \angle2, \angle6; \angle4, \angle8$

The relationships between parallel lines and their transversals can be used to justify the Triangle Sum Theorem. This theorem states that the sum of the angles of a triangle is 180°.

Extend the sides of the triangle to create transversals.

1. $\angle D$ and what angle are alternate interior angles? $\angle B$
2. Since these two angles are alternate interior angles, they are _congruent_
3. $\angle E$ and what angle are alternate interior angles? $\angle C$
4. Since these two angles are alternate interior angles, they are _congruent_ .
5. $\angle D$, $\angle A$, and $\angle E$ form a straight _line_ .
6. The angle measure of a straight line is _180°_, therefore $m\angle D + m\angle A + m\angle E = $ _180°_
7. Using the relationships from #3 and #5, find the sum: $m\angle A + m\angle B + m\angle C =$ _180°_
8. The sum of the angle measures in a triangle is always _180°_

Page 73

NAME _____

Lesson 5.5 Transversals and Calculating Angles

The relationships between parallel lines and their transversals can be used to justify the Exterior Angle Theorem. The Exterior Angle Theorem states that a measure of an exterior angle of a triangle is equal to the sum of the measures of the two non-adjacent interior angles.

Extend the sides of the triangle to create transversals.

What do $\angle C$ and $\angle D$ form? A straight line.

What is the sum of the measures for $\angle C$ and $\angle D$? 180°

Set the sum of the interior angles equal to the sum of $\angle C$ and $\angle D$ since they both equal 180°. Simplify the equation.

$$\angle A + \angle B + \angle C = \angle C + \angle D$$
$$\underline{\quad -\angle C \quad -\angle C \quad}$$
$$\angle A + \angle B = \angle D$$

The Exterior Angle Theorem states that the measure of an exterior angle is equal to the sum of its remote interior angles.

Find the measure of each interior angle of the triangle, if $\angle D = 105°$ and $\angle E = 65°$.

$$\angle B = \angle E = 65°$$
$$\angle C = 180 - 105 = 75°$$
$$\angle A + \angle B = 105° \rightarrow \angle A = 105 - 65 = 40°$$

Page 74

NAME _____

Lesson 5.6 Proving the Pythagorean Theorem

Use the image to answer the questions.

1. How are the squares related to the side of the triangle?

   The side length of the squares are the side lengths of the triangle.

2. How are the areas of the squares related?

   The sum of the area of the smaller squares is equal to the area of the largest square.

3. Write a general equation to represent the relationship that you described in #2.

   $$a^2 + b^2 = c^2$$

4. If you used the same model for a triangle with legs of 9 units and 12 units, what would be the area of the third square?

   $9^2 + 12^2 = c^2$
   $81 + 144 = 225$

   The area of the third square would be 225 square units.

Page 75

NAME _____

Lesson 5.7 Triangles in the Real World

A painter is painting a tall wall. He has a 20-foot ladder that is 4 feet from the base of the wall. Is the ladder long enough for him to reach a spot that is 15 feet high on the wall?

The wall, ground, and ladder form a right triangle, so you can use the Pythagorean Theorem to find the length of the missing side. The Pythagorean Theorem states that $a^2 + b^2 = c^2$, where a and b are the lengths of the legs of a right triangle, and c is the length of the hypotenuse.

The hypotenuse is the side of the triangle that is opposite the right angle in the triangle.

$$a = 4 \text{ feet}; b = 15 \text{ feet}$$
$$4^2 + 15^2 = c^2; 16 + 225 = c^2$$
$$241 = c^2; \sqrt{241} = \sqrt{c^2}$$
$$15.5 = c$$

The ladder is long enough. It only needs to be 15.5 feet long.

Answer the questions. Show your work.

Phoebe cut across the soccer field to get to the parking lot, rather than walk along the perimeter of the field. If the field is 100 yards long and 50 yards wide, how much distance did she save by cutting across the field?

If she walks along the perimeter:
100 yards + 50 yards = 150 yards
Diagonal:
$100^2 + 50^2 = c^2 \rightarrow 10000 + 2500 = c^2$
$12500 = c^2 \rightarrow \sqrt{12500} = \sqrt{c^2} \rightarrow c = 111.8$ yards
She saved $150 - 111.8 = 38.2$ yards

A pipe is being shipped in a long box that has a base of 2 ft. and a height of 8 ft. What is the longest length of pipe that can be shipped if it is put in the box diagonally?

$2^2 + 8^2 = c^2 \rightarrow 4 + 64 = c^2 \rightarrow 68 = c^2$
$\sqrt{68} = c \rightarrow c = 8.2$ feet

Answer Key

Page 76

NAME _____

Lesson 5.7 Triangles in the Real World

Answer the questions. Show your work.

Ronald and Donna both draw right triangles. The legs of Ronald's triangle are 4 cm and 5 cm. The legs of Donna's triangle are 3 cm and 6 cm. The sum of the legs of both their triangles is 9 centimeters, so they think that the hypotenuse of each of their triangles will be the same, too. Are they right?

Ronald   Donna

$4^2 + 5^2 = c^2$ $3^2 + 6^2 = c^2$
$16 + 25 = c^2$ $9 + 36 = c^2$
$41 = c^2$ No, they $45 = c^2$
$\sqrt{41} = \sqrt{c^2}$ are not right. $\sqrt{45} = \sqrt{c^2}$
$c = 6.4$ cm $c = 6.7$ cm

Twins Rolanda and Yolanda are tired of sharing their bedroom. They want to split their 12 feet by 15 feet room diagonally with a curtain that is 18 feet long. Is the curtain long enough?

$12^2 + 15^2 = c^2$
$144 + 225 = c^2$
$369 = c^2$
$\sqrt{369} = \sqrt{c^2}$
$c = 19.2$ ft.

The curtain is not long enough.

Spectrum Critical Thinking for Math
Grade 8
76

Lesson 5.7
Triangles in the Real World

Page 77

NAME _____

Lesson 5.8 Pythagorean Theorem and Distance

The Pythagorean Theorem can be used to find the distance between two points on a coordinate plane by using the horizontal and vertical distance between the points.

Find the distance between $(-5)^2 + 8^2 = c^2$; $25 + 64 = c^2$
the points (−2, 4) and (3, −4). $89 = c^2$; $\sqrt{89} = \sqrt{c^2}$
Horizontal distance: −2 − 3 = −5 $9.4 = c$
Vertical distance: 4 − (−4) = 8

Use the map to answer the questions. A side of each square represents 2 yards.

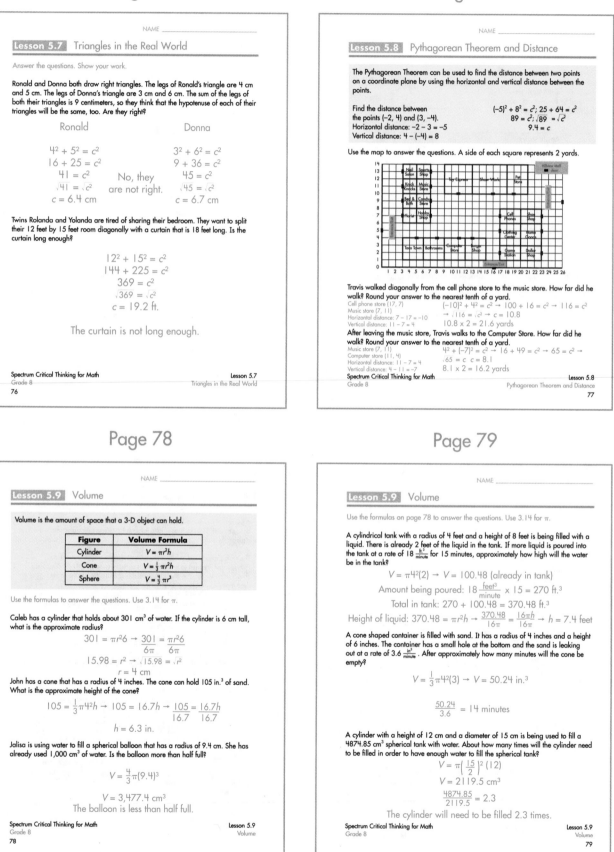

Travis walked diagonally from the cell phone store to the music store. How far did he walk? Round your answer to the nearest tenth of a yard.

Cell phone store (17, 7)
Music store (7, 11) $(-10)^2 + 4^2 = c^2 \rightarrow 100 + 16 = c^2 \rightarrow 116 = c^2$
Horizontal distance: 7 − 17 = −10 $\rightarrow \sqrt{116} = c^2 \rightarrow c = 10.8$
Vertical distance: 11 − 7 = 4 $10.8 \times 2 = 21.6$ yards

After leaving the music store, Travis walks to the Computer Store. How far did he walk? Round your answer to the nearest tenth of a yard.

Music store (7, 11)
Computer store (11, 4) $4^2 + (-7)^2 = c^2 \rightarrow 16 + 49 = c^2 \rightarrow 65 = c^2 \rightarrow$
Horizontal distance: 11 − 7 = 4 $\sqrt{65} = c = 8.1$
Vertical distance: 4 − 11 = −7 $8.1 \times 2 = 16.2$ yards

Spectrum Critical Thinking for Math
Grade 8

Lesson 5.8
Pythagorean Theorem and Distance
77

Page 78

NAME _____

Lesson 5.9 Volume

Volume is the amount of space that a 3-D object can hold.

Figure	Volume Formula
Cylinder	$V = \pi r^2 h$
Cone	$V = \frac{1}{3}\pi r^2 h$
Sphere	$V = \frac{4}{3}\pi r^3$

Use the formulas to answer the questions. Use 3.14 for π.

Caleb has a cylinder that holds about 301 cm³ of water. If the cylinder is 6 cm tall, what is the approximate radius?

$301 = \pi r^2 6 \rightarrow \frac{301}{6\pi} = \frac{\pi r^2 6}{6\pi}$
$15.98 = r^2 \rightarrow \sqrt{15.98} = \sqrt{r^2}$
$r = 4$ cm

John has a cone that has a radius of 4 inches. The cone can hold 105 in.³ of sand. What is the approximate height of the cone?

$105 = \frac{1}{3}\pi 4^2 h \rightarrow 105 = 16.7h \rightarrow \frac{105}{16.7} = \frac{16.7h}{16.7}$
$h = 6.3$ in.

Jalisa is using water to fill a spherical balloon that has a radius of 9.4 cm. She has already used 1,000 cm³ of water. Is the balloon more than half full?

$V = \frac{4}{3}\pi(9.4)^3$

$V = 3,477.4$ cm³
The balloon is less than half full.

Spectrum Critical Thinking for Math
Grade 8
78

Lesson 5.9
Volume

Page 79

NAME _____

Lesson 5.9 Volume

Use the formulas on page 78 to answer the questions. Use 3.14 for π.

A cylindrical tank with a radius of 4 feet and a height of 8 feet is being filled with a liquid. There is already 2 feet of the liquid in the tank. If more liquid is poured into the tank at a rate of 18 $\frac{ft.^3}{minute}$ for 15 minutes, approximately how high will the water be in the tank?

$V = \pi 4^2(2) \rightarrow V = 100.48$ (already in tank)

Amount being poured: $18 \frac{feet^3}{minute} \times 15 = 270$ ft.³

Total in tank: $270 + 100.48 = 370.48$ ft.³

Height of liquid: $370.48 = \pi r^2 h \rightarrow \frac{370.48}{16\pi} = \frac{16\pi h}{16\pi} \rightarrow h = 7.4$ feet

A cone shaped container is filled with sand. It has a radius of 4 inches and a height of 6 inches. The container has a small hole at the bottom and the sand is leaking out at a rate of 3.6 $\frac{in^3}{minute}$. After approximately how many minutes will the cone be empty?

$V = \frac{1}{3}\pi 4^2(3) \rightarrow V = 50.24$ in.³

$\frac{50.24}{3.6} = 14$ minutes

A cylinder with a height of 12 cm and a diameter of 15 cm is being used to fill a 4874.85 cm³ spherical tank with water. About how many times will the cylinder need to be filled in order to have enough water to fill the spherical tank?

$V = \pi\left(\frac{15}{2}\right)^2(12)$
$V = 2119.5$ cm³

$\frac{4874.85}{2119.5} = 2.3$

The cylinder will need to be filled 2.3 times.

Spectrum Critical Thinking for Math
Grade 8
79

Lesson 5.9
Volume

Answer Key

Page 80

NAME _____

Check What You Learned

Geometry

1. Help the game designer change the game scene.
   a. Move the Super Plus down 4 and right 3.
   b. Reflect the gym over the y-axis.
   c. Reflect the Eye of the Math Teacher over the x-axis and dilate by a scale of $\frac{1}{2}$.

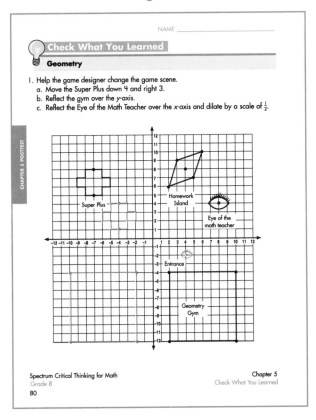

Page 81

NAME _____

Check What You Learned

Geometry

2. What are the measures of $\angle 1$, $\angle 2$, and $\angle 3$?

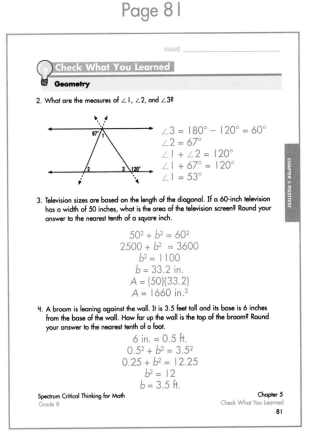

$\angle 3 = 180° - 120° = 60°$
$\angle 2 = 67°$
$\angle 1 + \angle 2 = 120°$
$\angle 1 + 67° = 120°$
$\angle 1 = 53°$

3. Television sizes are based on the length of the diagonal. If a 60-inch television has a width of 50 inches, what is the area of the television screen? Round your answer to the nearest tenth of a square inch.

$$50^2 + b^2 = 60^2$$
$$2500 + b^2 = 3600$$
$$b^2 = 1100$$
$$b = 33.2 \text{ in.}$$
$$A = (50)(33.2)$$
$$A = 1660 \text{ in.}^2$$

4. A broom is leaning against the wall. It is 3.5 feet tall and its base is 6 inches from the base of the wall. How far up the wall is the top of the broom? Round your answer to the nearest tenth of a foot.

$$6 \text{ in.} = 0.5 \text{ ft.}$$
$$0.5^2 + b^2 = 3.5^2$$
$$0.25 + b^2 = 12.25$$
$$b^2 = 12$$
$$b = 3.5 \text{ ft.}$$

Page 82

NAME _____

Check What You Learned

Geometry

5. Kobe wants to go to the gym with his friends. He started at Shaquille's house, then went to LeBron's house, and then went to the gym. If he traveled on a diagonal path, how far did he travel if each unit represents a city block? Round your answer to the nearest tenth.

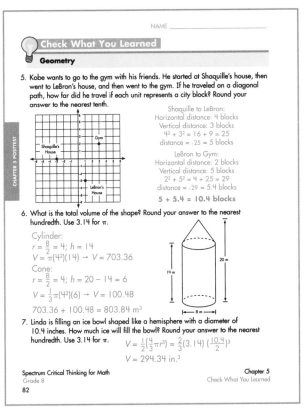

Shaquille to LeBron:
Horizontal distance: 4 blocks
Vertical distance: 3 blocks
$4^2 + 3^2 = 16 + 9 = 25$
distance $= \sqrt{25} = 5$ blocks

LeBron to Gym:
Horizontal distance: 2 blocks
Vertical distance: 5 blocks
$2^2 + 5^2 = 4 + 25 = 29$
distance $= \sqrt{29} = 5.4$ blocks

5 + 5.4 = 10.4 blocks

6. What is the total volume of the shape? Round your answer to the nearest hundredth. Use 3.14 for π.

Cylinder:
$r = \frac{8}{2} = 4$; $h = 14$
$V = \pi(4^2)(14) \rightarrow V = 703.36$
Cone:
$r = \frac{8}{2} = 4$; $h = 20 - 14 = 6$
$V = \frac{1}{3}\pi(4^2)(6) \rightarrow V = 100.48$

$703.36 + 100.48 = 803.84 \text{ m}^3$

7. Linda is filling an ice bowl shaped like a hemisphere with a diameter of 10.4 inches. How much ice will fill the bowl? Round your answer to the nearest hundredth. Use 3.14 for π.
$V = \frac{1}{2}\left(\frac{4}{3}\pi r^3\right) = \frac{2}{3}(3.14)\left(\frac{10.4}{2}\right)^3$
$V = 294.34 \text{ in.}^3$

Page 83

NAME _____

Check What You Know

Statistics and Probability

1. State whether the graphs show negative, positive, or no association.

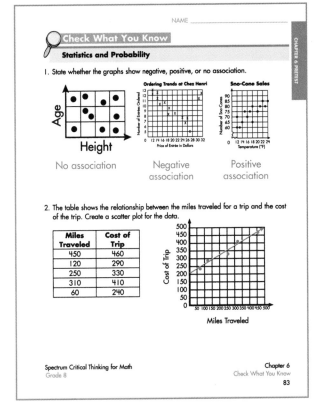

No association

Negative association

Positive association

2. The table shows the relationship between the miles traveled for a trip and the cost of the trip. Create a scatter plot for the data.

Miles Traveled	Cost of Trip
450	460
120	290
250	330
310	410
60	240

Answer Key

Page 84

CHAPTER 6 PRETEST

Check What You Know

Statistics and Probability

3. Draw a trend line.

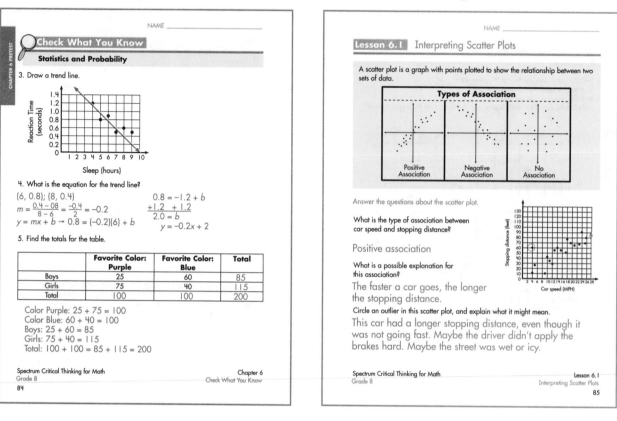

4. What is the equation for the trend line?

(6, 0.8); (8, 0.4)

$m = \frac{0.4 - 08}{8 - 6} = \frac{-0.4}{2} = -0.2$

$y = mx + b \rightarrow 0.8 = (-0.2)(6) + b$

$0.8 = -1.2 + b$
$+1.2 \quad +1.2$
$2.0 = b$

$y = -0.2x + 2$

5. Find the totals for the table.

	Favorite Color: Purple	Favorite Color: Blue	Total
Boys	25	60	85
Girls	75	40	115
Total	100	100	200

Color Purple: 25 + 75 = 100
Color Blue: 60 + 40 = 100
Boys: 25 + 60 = 85
Girls: 75 + 40 = 115
Total: 100 + 100 = 85 + 115 = 200

Page 85

Lesson 6.1 Interpreting Scatter Plots

A scatter plot is a graph with points plotted to show the relationship between two sets of data.

Types of Association

Positive Association | Negative Association | No Association

Answer the questions about the scatter plot.

What is the type of association between car speed and stopping distance?

Positive association

What is a possible explanation for this association?

The faster a car goes, the longer the stopping distance.

Circle an outlier in this scatter plot, and explain what it might mean.

This car had a longer stopping distance, even though it was not going fast. Maybe the driver didn't apply the brakes hard. Maybe the street was wet or icy.

Page 86

Lesson 6.2 Constructing a Scatter Plot

Use the table to create a scatter plot by graphing each ordered pair on the coordinate plane.

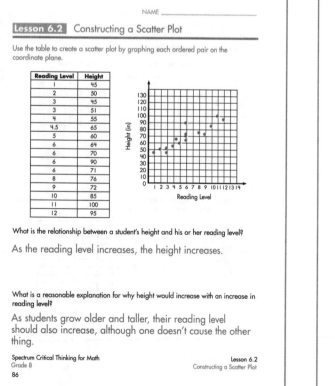

Reading Level	Height
1	45
2	50
3	45
3	51
4	55
4.5	65
5	60
6	64
6	70
6	90
6	71
8	76
9	72
10	85
11	100
12	95

What is the relationship between a student's height and his or her reading level?

As the reading level increases, the height increases.

What is a reasonable explanation for why height would increase with an increase in reading level?

As students grow older and taller, their reading level should also increase, although one doesn't cause the other thing.

Page 87

Lesson 6.3 Linear Models

A trend line shows the general direction that the points of a scatter plot seems to be going. The trend line of a scatter plot can be used to understand or make predictions about relationships between two variables.

Use the table to create a scatter plot by graphing each ordered pair on the coordinate plane. Draw a trend line through the data. Approximately half of the points should be above the line drawn, and the other half should be below it.

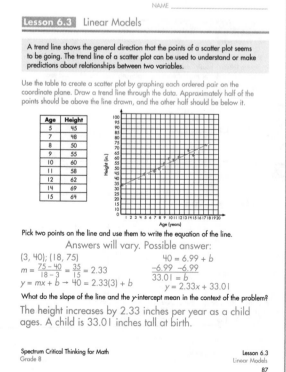

Age	Height
5	45
7	48
8	50
9	55
10	60
11	58
12	62
14	69
15	64

Pick two points on the line and use them to write the equation of the line.

Answers will vary. Possible answer:

(3, 40); (18, 75)

$m = \frac{75 - 40}{18 - 3} = \frac{35}{15} = 2.33$

$y = mx + b \rightarrow 40 = 2.33(3) + b$

$40 = 6.99 + b$
$-6.99 \quad -6.99$
$33.01 = b$

$y = 2.33x + 33.01$

What do the slope of the line and the y-intercept mean in the context of the problem?

The height increases by 2.33 inches per year as a child ages. A child is 33.01 inches tall at birth.

Answer Key

Page 88

Lesson 6.3 Linear Models

Use the table to create a scatter plot. Draw a trend line through the data. Approximately half of the points should be above the line drawn, and the other half should be below it.

Price	Buyers
$2	20
$4	19
$6	17
$8	13
$10	8
$12	2
$14	1
$15	0

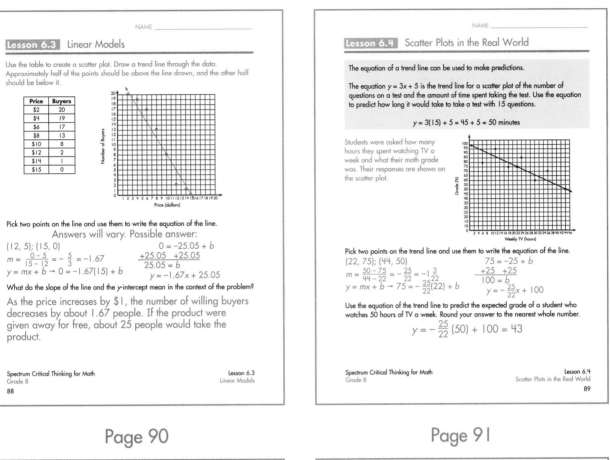

Pick two points on the line and use them to write the equation of the line.

Answers will vary. Possible answer:

$(12, 5); (15, 0)$

$m = \frac{0-5}{15-12} = -\frac{5}{3} = -1.67$

$y = mx + b \rightarrow 0 = -1.67(15) + b$

$0 = -25.05 + b$

$\frac{+25.05 \quad +25.05}{25.05 = b}$

$y = -1.67x + 25.05$

What do the slope of the line and the y-intercept mean in the context of the problem?

As the price increases by $1, the number of willing buyers decreases by about 1.67 people. If the product were given away for free, about 25 people would take the product.

Page 89

Lesson 6.4 Scatter Plots in the Real World

The equation of a trend line can be used to make predictions.

The equation $y = 3x + 5$ is the trend line for a scatter plot of the number of questions on a test and the amount of time spent taking the test. Use the equation to predict how long it would take to take a test with 15 questions.

$$y = 3(15) + 5 = 45 + 5 = 50 \text{ minutes}$$

Students were asked how many hours they spent watching TV a week and what their math grade was. Their responses are shown on the scatter plot.

Pick two points on the trend line and use them to write the equation of the line.

$(22, 75); (44, 50)$

$m = \frac{50-75}{44-22} = -\frac{25}{22} = -1\frac{3}{22}$

$y = mx + b \rightarrow 75 = -\frac{25}{22}(22) + b$

$75 = -25 + b$

$\frac{+25 \quad +25}{100 = b}$

$y = -\frac{25}{22}x + 100$

Use the equation of the trend line to predict the expected grade of a student who watches 50 hours of TV a week. Round your answer to the nearest whole number.

$$y = -\frac{25}{22}(50) + 100 = 43$$

Page 90

Lesson 6.4 Scatter Plots in the Real World

The average speeds of cars during the Friday rush hour were recorded. Data collection started at 4:30 PM. Use the scatter plot to answer the questions.

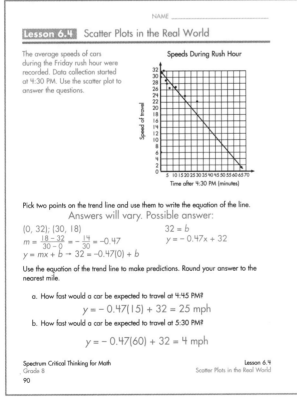

Speeds During Rush Hour

Pick two points on the trend line and use them to write the equation of the line.

Answers will vary. Possible answer:

$(0, 32); (30, 18)$

$m = \frac{18-32}{30-0} = -\frac{14}{30} = -0.47$

$y = mx + b \rightarrow 32 = -0.47(0) + b$

$32 = b$

$y = -0.47x + 32$

Use the equation of the trend line to make predictions. Round your answer to the nearest mile.

a. How fast would a car be expected to travel at 4:45 PM?

$$y = -0.47(15) + 32 = 25 \text{ mph}$$

b. How fast would a car be expected to travel at 5:30 PM?

$$y = -0.47(60) + 32 = 4 \text{ mph}$$

Page 91

Lesson 6.4 Scatter Plots in the Real World

Luis is training for a marathon. He records his mileage and time each day. Use the scatter plot to answer the questions.

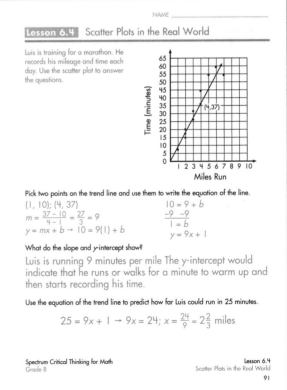

Pick two points on the trend line and use them to write the equation of the line.

$(1, 10); (4, 37)$

$m = \frac{37-10}{4-1} = \frac{27}{3} = 9$

$y = mx + b \rightarrow 10 = 9(1) + b$

$10 = 9 + b$

$\frac{-9 \quad -9}{1 = b}$

$y = 9x + 1$

What do the slope and y-intercept show?

Luis is running 9 minutes per mile The y-intercept would indicate that he runs or walks for a minute to warm up and then starts recording his time.

Use the equation of the trend line to predict how far Luis could run in 25 minutes.

$$25 = 9x + 1 \rightarrow 9x = 24; x = \frac{24}{9} = 2\frac{2}{3} \text{ miles}$$

Page 92

NAME _____

Lesson 6.5 Two-Way Tables

A two-way table shows data for two different categories. The table below shows the number of children who watch the TV shows "Dancing Stars" and "Zombie Nation."

	"Dancing Stars"	"Zombie Nation"	Total
Girls	30	10	40
Boys	5	25	30
Total	35	35	70

How many students are represented?
30 + 10 = 40 girls and 5 + 25 = 30 boys: a total of 70 students. OR:
30 + 5 = 35 watch "Dancing Stars" and 10 + 25 = 35 watch "Zombie Nation": a total of 70 students.

What percentage of students are boys who watch "Zombie Nation"? $\frac{25}{70}$ = 35.7%

	Chores	No Chores	Total
Curfew	32	8	40
No Curfew	2	8	10
Total	34	16	50

Use the two-way table to answer the questions.

Find the totals for the table.
Curfew: 32 + 8 = 40   No Curfew: 2 + 8 = 10
Chores: 32 + 2 = 34   No Chores: 8 + 8 = 16
Grand Total: 40 + 10 = 34 + 16 = 50
What percentage of students have no chores and no curfew?

$$\frac{8}{50} = 0.16 = 16\%$$

Page 93

NAME _____

Lesson 6.5 Two-Way Tables

Use the two-way table to answer the questions.

	Football	Basketball	Total
Allergies	14	26	40
No Allergies	31	9	40
Total	45	35	80

Find the totals for the table.
Allergies: 14 + 26 = 40   No Allergies: 31 + 9 = 40
Football: 14 + 31 = 45   Basketball: 26 + 9 = 35
Grand Total: 40 + 40 = 45 + 35 = 80

What percentage of students have allergies and like football?
$$\frac{14}{80} = 0.175 = 17.5\%$$

Create a frequency table with the following information:

Mr. Neeley interviewed 100 eighth graders to see if they had 200 or more songs on their smartphones. He also noted if the student was a girl or a boy. Of the students, 20% had less than 200 songs, 40% were boys, and 50% of the boys had 200 or more songs.

	Less than 200 songs	200 or more songs	Total
Boys	20	20	40
Girls	0	60	60
Total	20	80	100

Grand total: 100
Less than 200: 0.20 · 100 = 20 therefore, 80 have 200 or more songs
40% were boys: 0.40 · 100 = 40, therefore, 60 were girls
50% of the boys had 200 or more songs: 0.5 · 40 = 20, therefore 20 had less than 200
There were no girls with less than 200 since all of the 20 were boys.
There are 60 girls with 200 or more so we can bring the total with 200 or more to 80.

Page 94

NAME _____

💡 **Check What You Learned**

Statistics and Probability

A class collected data to see if there was a relationship between shoe size and height.

Shoe Size	Height
5	55
6	62
12	72
10	71
8	69
11	70
7	64
11	72

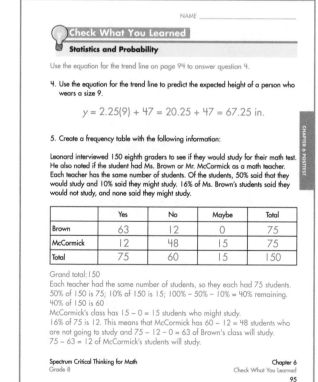

1. Create a scatter plot with the data.

2. What is the equation of the trend line for this scatter plot?
Answers will vary. Possible answer:
(0, 47); (8, 65)   47 = b
$m = \frac{65 - 47}{8 - 0} = \frac{18}{8} = 2.25$ y = 2.25x + 47
y = mx + b → 47 = 2.25(0) + b

3. What do the slope and y-intercept of the scatter plot represent?
The slope means that the height changes by 2.25 inches as the shoe size increases by 1. The y-intercept means that the height of someone before they get into a size 1 is 47 inches.

CHAPTER 6 POSTTEST

Page 95

NAME _____

💡 **Check What You Learned**

Statistics and Probability

Use the equation for the trend line on page 94 to answer question 4.

4. Use the equation for the trend line to predict the expected height of a person who wears a size 9.

$$y = 2.25(9) + 47 = 20.25 + 47 = 67.25 \text{ in.}$$

5. Create a frequency table with the following information:

Leonard interviewed 150 eighth graders to see if they would study for their math test. He also noted if the student has Ms. Brown or Mr. McCormick as a math teacher. Each teacher has the same number of students. Of the students, 50% said that they would study and 10% said they might study. 16% of Ms. Brown's students said they would not study, and none said they might study.

	Yes	No	Maybe	Total
Brown	63	12	0	75
McCormick	12	48	15	75
Total	75	60	15	150

Grand total: 150
Each teacher had the same number of students, so they each had 75 students.
50% of 150 is 75; 10% of 150 is 15; 100% − 50% − 10% = 40% remaining.
40% of 150 is 60
McCormick's class has 15 − 0 = 15 students who might study.
16% of 75 is 12. This means that McCormick has 60 − 12 = 48 students who are not going to study and 75 − 12 − 0 = 63 of Brown's class will study.
75 − 63 = 12 of McCormick's students will study.

CHAPTER 6 POSTTEST

Answer Key

Page 96

NAME _____

Check What You Learned

Statistics and Probability

	With Toppings	No Toppings	Total
Vanilla Ice Cream	9	8	17
Chocolate Ice Cream	7	9	16
Total	16	17	33

Use the two-way table to answer the questions.

6. Find the totals for the table.
   Vanilla: 9 + 8 = 17   Chocolate: 7 + 9 = 16
   With Toppings: 9 + 7 = 16   No Toppings: 8 + 9 = 17
   Total: 17 + 16 = 16 + 17 = 33

7. What percentage of students like vanilla with no toppings? Round your answer to the nearest percent.

$$\frac{8}{33} = 0.24 = 24\%$$

8. Create a frequency table with the following information:

Mrs. Rakes interviewed 100 eighth graders to see if they preferred bowling or skating. She also noted if the student was a girl or a boy. Of the students, 42% like bowling, 48% were boys, and 25% of the boys preferred bowling.

	Skating	Bowling	Total
Boys	36	12	48
Girls	22	30	52
Total	58	42	100

Spectrum Critical Thinking for Math
Grade 8
96

Chapter 6
Check What You Learned

CHAPTER 6 POSTTEST

Page 97

NAME _____

Final Test Chapters 1–6

Answer the questions. Show your work.

1. Shanise has 12 cubes that measure 12 units on each side. She says that the total volume of the cubes is 12×12^3. Juan disagrees and says that the total volume is 12^4. Who is correct?

$$12 \cdot 12^3 = 12^{1+3} = 12^4$$
They are both correct.

2. The number of foreign travelers who visited New York City was 4.0×10^6 and the number that visited Boston was 7.2×10^5. How many times greater was the number of New York travelers than the number of Boston travelers? Round your answer to the nearest tenth.

$$\frac{4.0 \times 10^6}{7.2 \times 10^5} = \left(\frac{4.0}{7.2}\right) \times 10^{6-5} =$$
$$0.56 \times 10 =$$
$$5.6 \times 10^0 = 5.6$$

3. Which is greater: $\sqrt{35}$ or $5\sqrt{7}$?

$\sqrt{25} < \sqrt{35} < \sqrt{36}$ $\sqrt{4} < \sqrt{7} < \sqrt{9}$
$5 < \sqrt{35} < 6$ $2 < \sqrt{7} < 3$
$35 - 25 = 10; 36 - 25 = 11$ $7 - 4 = 3; 9 - 4 = 5$
$\frac{10}{11} = 0.91 \rightarrow 5 + 0.91 = 5.91$ $\frac{3}{5} = 0.6 \rightarrow 2 + 0.6 = 2.6 \times 5 = 13$

$$5\sqrt{7} > \sqrt{35}$$

4. A square table cloth has an area of 1,600 square inches. It is placed on a table that has an area of 1,200 square inches. How much of the table cloth will hang over on each side? Round your answer to the nearest tenth of an inch.

Table sides: $\sqrt{1200} = 34.6$
Table cloth sides: $\sqrt{1600} = 40$
There will be $40 - 34.6 = 5.4$ inches on each side length
$\frac{5.4}{2} = 2.7$ inches will hang on each side of the table.

Spectrum Critical Thinking for Math
Grade 8

Chapters 1–6
Final Test
97

CHAPTERS 1–6 FINAL TEST

Page 98

NAME _____

Final Test Chapters 1–6

5. The iGo service charges a $10 fee to pick up a customer, and $0.10 per mile. uGo car service has no pickup fee, but charges $0.35 per mile. Find the number of miles for which the cost of both services is the same.

iGo: $c = 10 + 0.10m$; uGo: $c = 0.35m$
$10 + 0.10m = 0.35m$
$10 = 0.25m \rightarrow m = 40$
The cost will be the same for 40 miles.

6. Harry is saving up for a game that costs $75. He has $28 in the bank. He saves $12 a week. The equation $s = 12w + 28$ represents how much he has saved after w weeks. How long will it take for him to earn enough for the game? Round your answer to the nearest week.

$$75 = 12w + 28$$
$$\underline{-28 \qquad -28}$$
$$47 = 12w$$
$$3.92 = w$$
It would take 4 weeks.

7. Does this equation have one solution, no solution, or infinitely many solutions?

$-3(x + 4) = -12 - 3x$

$$-3(x + 4) = -12 - 3x$$
$$-3x - 12 = -12 - 3x$$
$$\underline{+3x \qquad\qquad +3x}$$
$$-12 = -12$$
Infinitely many solutions.

8. Does this equation have one solution, no solution, or infinitely many solutions?

$5(x - 2) + 3 = 5x - 9$

$$5(x - 2) + 3 = 5x - 9$$
$$5x - 10 + 3 = 5x - 9$$
$$5x - 7 = 5x - 9$$
$$-7 = -9$$
No solution.

Spectrum Critical Thinking for Math
Grade 8
98

Chapters 1–6
Final Test

CHAPTERS 1–6 FINAL TEST

Page 99

NAME _____

Final Test Chapters 1–6

9. The graph below represents the speed of a car over a given amount of time. Which section(s) of the graph represents a constant speed?

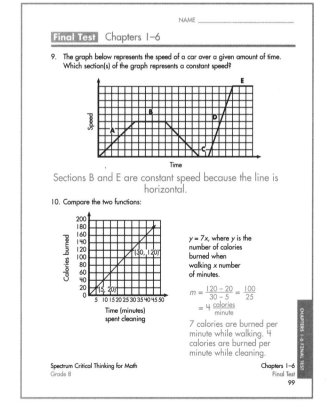

Sections B and E are constant speed because the line is horizontal.

10. Compare the two functions:

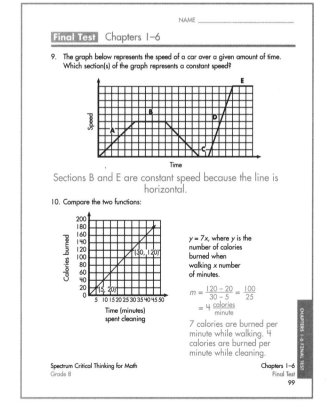

$y = 7x$, where y is the number of calories burned when walking x number of minutes.

$m = \frac{120 - 20}{30 - 5} = \frac{100}{25}$
$= 4 \frac{calories}{minute}$

7 calories are burned per minute while walking. 4 calories are burned per minute while cleaning.

Spectrum Critical Thinking for Math
Grade 8

Chapters 1–6
Final Test
99

CHAPTERS 1–6 FINAL TEST

Page 100

NAME _____

Final Test Chapters 1–6

11. What effect does a translation of $(x - 8, y + 10)$ have on the perimeter of a triangle?

A translation doesn't change the shape and size of the shape. The perimeter is the same.

12. What are the coordinates of a triangle with vertices A $(-1, 2)$; B $(8, -9)$; and C $(6, 1)$ after a rotation 90° clockwise about the origin?

$(y, -x)$
A $(-1, 2) \rightarrow$ A'$(2, 1)$
B $(8, -9) \rightarrow$ B'$(-9, -8)$
C $(6, 1) \rightarrow$ C'$(1, -6)$

13. Find the value of each angle of the triangle.

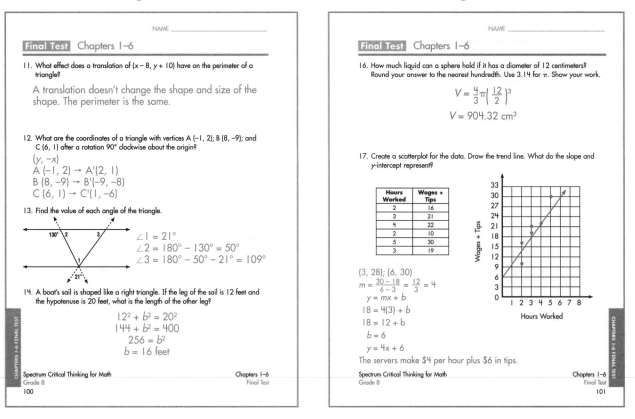

$\angle 1 = 21°$
$\angle 2 = 180° - 130° = 50°$
$\angle 3 = 180° - 50° - 21° = 109°$

14. A boat's sail is shaped like a right triangle. If the leg of the sail is 12 feet and the hypotenuse is 20 feet, what is the length of the other leg?

$12^2 + b^2 = 20^2$
$144 + b^2 = 400$
$256 = b^2$
$b = 16$ feet

CHAPTERS 1-6 FINAL TEST

Spectrum Critical Thinking for Math
Grade 8
100

Chapters 1–6
Final Test

Page 101

NAME _____

Final Test Chapters 1–6

16. How much liquid can a sphere hold if it has a diameter of 12 centimeters? Round your answer to the nearest hundredth. Use 3.14 for π. Show your work.

$$V = \frac{4}{3}\pi \left(\frac{12}{2} \right)^3$$
$$V = 904.32 \text{ cm}^3$$

17. Create a scatterplot for the data. Draw the trend line. What do the slope and y-intercept represent?

Hours Worked	Wages + Tips
2	16
3	21
4	22
2	10
5	30
3	19

$(3, 28); (6, 30)$
$m = \frac{30 - 18}{6 - 3} = \frac{12}{3} = 4$
$y = mx + b$
$18 = 4(3) + b$
$18 = 12 + b$
$b = 6$
$y = 4x + 6$

The servers make $4 per hour plus $6 in tips.

CHAPTERS 1-6 FINAL TEST

Spectrum Critical Thinking for Math
Grade 8
101

Chapters 1–6
Final Test

Notes

Notes